Does
God
Need
Glasses

Evil
And
Genesis

Richard Mure
Exelby

*Sajmište Monument on the site of
the Nazi Concentration Camp on
the banks of the Sava at Belgrade,
Serbia, in memory of the estimated 23ooo Serbians and Jews who
died there.*

e-book: ISBN 978-82-691244-1-5   printed: ISBN 978-82-691244-0-8

Foreword

"If God could look at a world like ours,
and call it "very good",
- then He must need glasses!"

This book has slowly developed since its first inspiration on a sunny Sunday afternoon in early spring when I was a student. No longer an atheist -I had learned to know the God who is There the year before, I was sitting in a secluded area of the UEA University Village, studying the Bible Creation Story with fresh eyes, and to my amazement found:

It solved the Problem of Evil!

The Problem of Evil is supposed to be unanswerable. This book is a summary of what I saw, and the implications of the answer I found there.

There may still be many issues to address and to some the answer may seem all too simple. But there again, E= mc^2 is a very simple equation. Does that make it wrong? Whether an answer to something is adequate for you or not depends on what questions you struggle with -and as they could be legion, it would be stupid for me to claim to give all the answers. You must judge for yourself whether what I propose here is helpful -or what is more important: right.

The ideas here have also been summarised in a video series on YouTube. These may clear up one or two things not explained fully here. I have put links to these at various places in the text and at the end of this document.

The Problem

In a world of pain and heartache everywhere.

Do you ever feel you're drowning in despair?

Don't give in, take some time to praise His Name.

And you will feel the burden lift away;

(Steve Camp: "It is Good")

Does God need glasses?

How else could He look at a world like ours and call it "very good" unless He can't see straight? Do His eyes need testing?

All the

starvation and disease,

suffering and violence,

theft and robbery,

human trafficking,

lust for power,

intolerance, cheating,

exploitation and wallowing in wealth -side by side with starvation!

Can God not see it? And -if there is one- who made the Devil?

How can a God of Love make a world so bad? Is He a sadist or indifferent or downright impotent? Is the Bible contradicting itself when it claims this world was made by an all-powerful, loving God?

This, in a nutshell, is the age-old question we call the Problem of Evil: "Can God be Almighty, Good, and the Creator of everything, while the world is so patently ill?"

Yes: He can! God truly is good says the Bible, and it shows an answer that is profoundly practical yet intellectually cohesive. It is one of the first questions the it deals with. Moreover, the Bible follows the matter through from start to finish. But God is far more concerned with doing away with evil in practice, than in slaking our philosophical curiosity. To paraphrase Karl Marx: What really matters, is not "*how to understand where evil comes from*" but **how to get rid of it!**[1]

So what the world needs to know is that God does not delight in

tears...

or death,

...neither sorrow,

...nor crying,

...nor pain,[2]

and one day He will put an end to them all. God *is* doing something about Evil![3]

Nor does God need glasses, He truly is Almighty, Creator of all things and steadfast Love.

Child's Play?

The Bible starts with two stories that seem like child's play. Believe me, they are anything but! They are parables packing a heavy philosophical punch that is extremely radical, and still relevant today. We call them the Creation Stories.

Treat them as child's play and you will overlook the point, -especially if you think you know them already. Very likely what you are actually thinking of is not the real thing; more likely you are remembering the distorted folk-lore version about apples or a 'tree of knowledge'. Infant's School may be the first place you heard it, but this tale is as far a cry from the kindergarten as gold from gilding.

 Ancient peoples explained their philosophy and world-view through poetic parables -tales with a deeper meaning, not academic discussions and intellectual dialogues. The first key to a myth is: take the story seriously and after that, plumb its depths. Key number two is read it on its own premises; otherwise you can totally misread what it has to say.

The Creation accounts in the Bible are ancient literature for people of ancient times told in a way they could understand: the myth. But they have a timelessness about them. Modern readers get the point too, and can apply their relevance to themselves. So the genre of the story is the same as myths of other ancient cultures like Sumer and draws on them.[4] However, it says something different. Similarities to other creation myths of the same period are interesting enough, but can throw us off the scent. The Creation accounts have a distinctive message.

Chaos is the true primaeval state of the other myths. In other words, the forces that bring about existence are random, and happen due to an impersonal process with no purpose or cohesion. Chaos then throws up the gods spontaneously and they organise chaos into a material world.[5]

The gods are often at war with one another. So the message you find in the polytheistic myth is that the universe is fragmented and sometimes self-contradictory. If there is a unifying factor, some high god like Wotan, Zeus or Vishnu ruling all the rest, it is remote, unreachable and sometimes in conflict with the other gods.

According to the myths, personal forces (the gods) only come on the stage late in the game and are not the origin of reality itself. And these gods are capricious and sometimes not very friendly. The Greek gods, for example, put all the evils of this world in a box without a lock. The plan was to trap the first woman (Pandora) into opening it. When she did, out flew pain, sickness and sorrow. The gods *wanted* us to suffer, to keep us in our place and bring us to heel.[6]

In Hinduism, for example, all existence is Vishnu's dream. While he dreams, the dreams become the gods and the material world. If he ever wakes up, all will disintegrate. What is the message here? - Dreams are random and uncontrollable and sometimes puzzling, leading nowhere. Other times they seem sensible, but take odd twists and feel as if their meaning is hidden -if they have one. So the message is: we are not the product of purposeful cogitation. Life just happened to happen. All is directionless and unwilled.

So in the view of the myth-makers, we are reality's toys. In the final instance reality is impersonal and unconcerned with our well-being.

The Hebrew Creation Story is uncompromisingly counter-cultural. The Bible asserts that all existence is unified and begins with God. It is monotheistic in a polytheistic culture telling of One God, who is personal and works to a conscious, intelligent plan.

And there *are* only two possibilities anyway, ultimately: Either things were planned or they jus' 'growed'[7]. The cause of our existence is either personal -or impersonal! The rest is merely a discussion of the mechanics.[8]

The Bible opens with this:

"In the beginning God created the heaven and the earth"

God alone is the origin. All existence, and time, begin at His behest.[9] To put it a modern way: God brings the material universes[10] into being and sets off the Big Bang. The only "primaeval state" is God Himself - even chaos is His invention. The driving force of all Reality is *personal*.

The truly important question to answer is then:

"What does the Creation Story actually say?" and "Is it true?"

"Behold, it was very good!"

- God said "Let there be light!"

- and saw that it was good.

- "sky the dry land, the seas!"

- and saw that it was good.

- "grass, plants, trees!"

- and saw that it was good.

- "stars, sun and moon!"

- and saw that it was good.

- He created whales, fish and birds

- and saw that it was good.

- He brought forth every animal

- and saw that it was good.

- And made mankind in His own image,

  and seeing everything He had made:

- Behold, it was very good!

Count how many times "good" was said and you find "*It was good*" is systematically repeated and reaches its final culmination at "*Very Good*". Seven times, all counted.

In Hebrew writing,[11] seven is a typical number for "divine perfection". So "seven times good" means the created universe was more than good -it was completed -all it was meant to be: Six plus One = Seven = Perfect!

Humankind are included in the "everything" God sees is "very good". So they are only pronounced "*good*" in relation to Creation as a whole, not in isolation.[12] Possibly this is because of us having a unique task in the overall scheme of things: our "goodness" is baked into our place in the whole result.

However, since *everything* God had made was good, there **was** no Evil. Where does Evil come from then?

The clue lies in the next section: The Family Tree.

A Family Tree

A Map of Relationships

Genesis started with a timeline; telling things in the order they happened.

It now goes on to a new account showing the creation process in the form of a *Family Tree or genealogy* (which is another typical kind of ancient literature). This part is sometimes called the "Second Account of Creation".

The important thing about family trees is that they chart out *relationships*. For this reason, family trees can hop like a squirrel backwards and forwards in the timeline. Events are *not* told in strict chronological order but in their order of relevance. The tale may follow the elder son or daughter's line up to the present, go back to the beginning again, and then go off on a tangent to tell an anecdote about some colourful personality. They answer questions like: Who is the son of daughter of whom? How are these two individuals related? What happened in their lives?

It is not usual to call the second Creation Account "a family tree" so I need to explain what tells us it is one. The clue lies in the words *"these are the generations of"*

This phrase[13] gives rise to the name for the whole book: "Genesis" (the Greek for "origins")[14]. Every time this particular wording is used in the Old Testament (12 in all,) it is without exception used elsewhere about what is told *afterwards*. And what follows is a genealogy (a list of names, family relationships and anecdotes).

Just as a pound sign tells us we are calculating in UK money, not US dollars, or a Euro sign shows we are not using Yen,[15] so the heading shows us the *kind* of writing that follows and how to read it; For a family tree does not work like a timeline but a *map*!

The Creation Family Tree tells us how...

- God is related to humankind,

- Human beings are related to the earth they are made of,

- How animals, man and woman are all related to one another.

- What humankind is here for.

If you overlook the fundamental distinction between a timeline and a family tree you can easily tie yourself up in knots. You try in vain to synchronise the "first" and the "second" Creation Accounts,[16] or even think they contra-

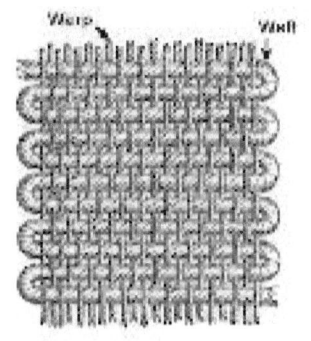

dict each other, but as the two versions are complementary that conclusion is flawed. The different angles of approach fill out the gaps in the other version just like in weaving: half the threads go downwards and the others go across.

God's purpose is not to stuff our heads with knowledge but bring us into a living 3-D relationship with Himself[17]. The Bible therefore often throws its light by showing the same thing from more than one side. Stories are repeated in a subtly different way and each illustration is valuable in its own right but highlights a different aspect. As we meditate on the versions and the connections and variations, this sets off an important process inside us. Our grasp changes from a two-dimensional relationship to words on paper to a three-dimensional encounter with the Living Reality beyond them.[18]

When you take the information from the Family Tree and weave it into the Timeline you then make some fascinating discoveries.

A Bit of Earth Showing Who God Is

The Red One

The word for humankind is "Adam" in Hebrew, "*the red one*"[19] and may refer to the reddish colour of terra-cotta pottery or of soil. "Adam" could mean a male *or* a female; the word takes masculine grammatical gender so translations will use "he" and "him" about the "adam" when we would say "it" -which can mislead you.[20] Later on, in the Family Tree, "Adam" is used as a proper name for the first man, but in the earlier timeline it simply means "human".

The verb "formed", is used for what God does when making both the "adam" and the animals. It is the same word used about making a vase or bowl at the potter's wheel. "Formed" gives the impression that an outside agency has pushed and pulled raw material into shape. So the "adam" went through a transformation before ending up the way the potter wanted.[21] In other words, the Creation story does not necessarily clash with the Theory of Evolution.[22]

Yet although "the adam" is clay, it is a pot containing the spirit of God: the breath of life is breathed in and it becomes a living creature for God to communicate with and give instructions.[23]

Genesis maps the relationship between God and us: We are designed to be like Him but there is a difference. We are the work of art, He the artist. An artist is flesh-and-blood, a self-portrait, lifeless pigments on canvas. But canvas and colours are an expression of the painter. So too, we humans express the nature of God - who is Spirit[24] but are composed of matter. We are literally "earthlings": shaped out of the dust of the earth like Ming vases, for it is *this* universe that is to reflect its Creator[25] *not* some outside element, *not* some "parallel spiritual visitor" put inside of us. This is an important point, for if the material universe could only express God by the input of an "exterior element" it would not be truly His.

Moreover, the universe needs to reflect God's own nature or else it will be out of kilter with God Himself[26] and out of line with the principles governing its own existence. The God of the Bible is not some impersonal force.[27] He is personal: thinking; living; feeling; active; self-determining; creative. What He makes in His image will be naturally be in keeping. So even if our universe reflects God's grandness, His infinite intelligence, His inventiveness and might, the Cosmos will still lack the absolutely most vital side to God if it does not also express His foremost personal quality:

-God is Love![28]

So the Creator makes humans to reflect and impart this Love. We are God's self-portrait, equipped with the same capacity to love[29] and have the task of administering, developing and ruling Gods world with His Love and through His Love. We are also made to be at the receiving end of love, too: We are Love's agents, transmitting Gods love everywhere -which includes ourselves.

Humankind
-Keystone of the Arch

The implications have enormous consequences for our self-understanding. So we need to look into them before we go on to consider the origin of Evil.

Firstly: *you are the product of intelligent deliberation.* You are not the chance result of some random process of adaptation to random circumstances: God said "let us make".

Secondly: *you have a role to play*: As you are in God's image, you demarcate the lordship of God wherever you are. The expression "image" refers to the statues or sculptures kings would put up in ancient times to show "this is my territory"!

Thirdly: *you are meant to bring a creative input of your own* into the world. Man plays a role of sub-creator.[30] The animals are similar to the Man, formed the same way and receiving the same "breath of life" but the Man is the leader: God *"brought (the animals) to the man to see what he would name them"* (name-giving implies leadership);[31] God does not tell Adam the names, *"whatever the man called each living creature, that was its name.*" Man makes the names up himself and decides the matter:

So latent within you, you have an active creativity meant to be contributed in fellowship with God (in the original plan of things). This is not some "never-to-be-strayed-from-pre-determined-track rigidly laid down" but a freely open-ended invitation to wander where you will. And to a certain extent this invitation still stands.[32]

This explains why we humans have more impact on the environment than any other animal on the planet. We are not a "foreign body in the eye of Nature"[33] -our creative input was meant to be part and parcel of the ecological balance. (Our later abuse of the role is a different story.)

Adam is taken and put in the Garden of Eden, a protected environment.[34] This is the reverse of evolutionism: We do not adapt to this environment, it is tailor-made for us.[35] But something is missing.

Welcome to the world, ladies: You make it perfect!

*"It is **not good** that the man is alone. I will make a help suitable for him."[36]*

Something is "Not-Good". The words stand out in stark contrast to the *"-and saw that it was good-"* repeated all the way to Perfection. This is because a vital bit is not in place yet.

Man met all the animals but though they were suitable as companions,[37] the parade only emphasised how not one single one of them was his match, something was lacking. So God brings forth Woman, and the universe takes a quantum leap.[38] Once Eve is created, God looks for the seventh time upon His handiwork and now He calls it: **"Perfect!"**

The Best was kept till last! If Man is head of creation, then Woman is the Crown! "Not-Good" has become "Thoroughly Good" and the creation of Eve brought about the change. How?

She can have babies: Eve makes the world dynamic!

Woman is as equally in the image of God as Man.39 Creating the man first does not have to mean subordinate importance but that all humanity springs from both sources combined (more of which below). Eve is equally endowed with abundant God-given talents, faculties and abilities. Some are the same as the man's; others are their complement. So she has a different perspective from his and a different take on priorities. This means that on joining forces, Man plus Woman tackle and achieve things neither will manage on their own -which is the point of marriage.40 However, neither Woman nor Man exist simply in order to have babies; that is is only one of the outcomes.41 We all exist for our own sake: to be at the receiving end of God's love.

But the name "Eve" (meaning "life" "*because she is mother of all living*",) is given to the Woman because she can have children. She adds a new element: God's Perfect universe is not static.

An endless flow of individuals will spring from the original couple.42 No two will be exactly alike; all will be diverse in personality and appearance. A simple origin will bring about our entire human race: "all the families of the world"; multiple, rich, and constantly throwing up subtle variations.

Like the many facets of a precious jewel, the image of God is both individual *and* collective. Every surface displays the many excellences of the Godhead in their slightly different way and all of them make up part of the whole. Each bit helps to complete the picture, like the many and varied stones of a mosaic. It is not that the image of God in humankind is incomplete -but our appreciation of it is! Grasping and appreciating that picture is an on-going affair just as humanity itself is an on-going affair.

> So *You Matter!* Without you, something is not there that should be.

This too has important bearings on your self-understanding: Since every one of us is formed in the image of God, *each one of us has significance in our own right.* Therefore: *You have a valid reason to accept and love yourself.*

But since every person highlights the Almighty uniquely, you then have a valid reason for not only valuing your *own* individuality but the uniqueness of *others, appreciating everyone for who they truly are.*

Love means relationships, so relationships also display God's Image, and they matter. Humans are therefore also created for relationships: The Man loves his Woman; the Woman loves her Man; they both love the children springing from their joyful love.

Eve is created *in relation to* Adam on purpose to illustrate their kinship, closeness and to reflect the love found within the Trinity. Woman issues from the closest side of the Man, she is *"bone of his bone and flesh of his flesh"* and becomes *"the mother of all living"* -just as the Holy Spirit issues *from* God, *is* God, and is *"the Lord, the giver of life."*[43]

*"In His image created He **him**; male and female created He **them**."*[44]

What God considers "Perfect" is therefore not something static. Perfection includes constantly renewed variations upon a theme that was perfect from the start.

This is at loggerheads with the idea of perfection that our western world has uncritically inherited from the Greeks, who considered anything material per definition as imperfect.[45] Greek "Perfection" was static and uniform and everyone was judged by how close they got to an ideal stereotype -those who didn't make the grade were:

"Losers! losers!"[46]

In God's world there is not *one* perfection but many - just as God Himself is infinite. Biblical "perfection" has no need to *strive* for perfection - it starts there! Right from the beginning God's world was complete and correct and the way it ought to be.

To use a numerical analogy: Hebrew "Perfection" is like the number Seven. It can be written small or large, many times or singly, in different inks, colours and writing-systems. No two examples need be alike but all are still 'seven'. God's perfect world could produce ever new varieties -like the multiplicity of the fractal-[47] all unique and every one as good and valid as the one before. The perfection of each new edition sprang from a total harmony and *"God.. ..made everything beautiful in its time."*[48].

So the world Genesis portrays was never intended as a 'Grand Fossilised Monument' to the creativity of God. Neither static nor uniform; its perfection included transition, going onwards from glory to glory.

At the Summit

The whole point of arriving at perfection
is to *stay* there.

From the top of a mountain all paths lead down. There is nothing to be gained by leaving God's kind of perfection: it is the launching pad for everything else. The Universe lay ready to release ever more exciting variations and possibilities to explore. But abandon perfection and all that is lost.

Now the "mountain" ("Creation", figuratively speaking), was Good all the way through. If you decide to go

down a mountain, there will be less under your feet than before - less Goodness. If you get all the way down to the bottom, then there will be no Goodness beneath you at all. You will also be as far from perfection as you can get.

But when you are halfway down, the mountain remaining below you is still "Good". However, you have wandered away from perfection. If you call the distance from the top "Evil", you will now be at a place that is a mix of the two: good below, Evil (-the lack in hight) above you. The place you are at now is "Good-and-Evil". (At the bottom, of course, then you will only be left with total Evil, which won't really happen for reasons I will go into later.)

So God's command meant *"stay at the top and never leave it"*: 'Keep with perfection!' 'Don't wander off down into the in-between realm of good-and-evil!'

But leaving the "mountain-top" was more drastic than you might think. It didn't just involve going down and then back up again. The Fall involved (as we shall see later,) blasting away the entire top of the mountain!

What now is left is still good but there's less of it than before, and you can't go back up to a mountain-top that is no longer there.

Here lies a clue to how Evil is created and what it is: Evil is a detraction from Perfection.

When an essential bit of creation is taken away, Evil arises in the vacuum left behind.[49] From then on we are stuck at a place that is "Good-and-Evil"[50].

"of the tree of the knowledge-of-good-and-evil you shall not eat"

Choices in a Perfect World

Read the Bible from cover to cover

- *and you will **not** find a 'tree of knowledge'.*

Read the Bible from cover to cover

- *and you will **not** find an 'apple tree'.*

- *We have read something into the Creation Story that isn't there:*

The 'tree of knowledge' is a figment of our imagination!

A fruit tree is a very loaded image in the Bible: it is the source or origin of something.[51] So the physical ability to choose between different trees, reflected an ability to investigate various aspects of life and get to know them.[52]

"Of every tree of the garden you may freely eat;" (apart from the one). The trees of the garden show that Perfection was a world not only of food, but of endless possibilities, experiences and knowledge (!!) all for our delight. It is, of course, only possible to "freely eat" when you have a free will, i.e. an autonomous power of choice.[53] But here the choices were all good and there was an open invitation to follow all and any of them in whatever order we felt like.

To put it figuratively, humankind could eat nothing but bananas the rest of their lives or sample every kind of fruit in turn; all the choices were good and none mutually exclusive.[54] Beyond the garden would be a similar vast ocean of choice for this was only the beginning. Ahead lay the blessing *"be fruitful and multiply; fill all the earth and subdue it;"*

There *are* no evil choices to make

- in an entirely good world,

- made by a good God

- and populated by good humankind

- unless one chooses to destroy an essential element first!

What, then, will happen if you do? The clue is given in the creation of Woman: Without Eve you regress to a mixture of "Good-and-Not-Good". However, we are talking now of "Not-Good" created by choice. We are dealing with the deliberate destruction of that original perfection. This is no longer a matter of things being uncompleted: it is done on purpose so it has a moral dimension: -it is Evil!

Evil is a choice deliberately to create "Not-Good".

The result? - ***Good-and-Evil***!

So what was God forbidding us to do?

-Destroy Perfection!

Forbidding the tree was not an arbitrary prohibition, not a random test, and not a petty way for God to assert His Godhood, -as if *anything* we could do or achieve would be able to threaten the maker of a universe so vast! It meant 'Do not impair perfection!'

Our creative input was not to be used in a way that damaged the Total Goodness of God's world. Eating the Forbidden Fruit would destroy something vital.

This is why Adam was told:

*"of the tree of the **knowledge-of-good-and-evil** you shall **not** eat,*

for in the day you eat of it, dying you shall die"[55]

("you shall start to die and end up dead!")

Rip out an essential part of Total Goodness and you bring about an unwanted and *compound state* of the universe: it becomes a mix of "**good-and-evil**".

Take a brilliantly woven tapestry and rip a hole in it. The tapestry is still brilliant but the gaping hole spoils it. The tapestry is now a mix of beauty-and-emptiness.

Remove the atmosphere and all life on the planet will be thrown into disruption: - the air needed by the rest has gone! The animals and plants are good (until the rot sets in) but the void left behind chokes everything; the absence of air is 'evil'.

Take a perfectly working machine made of pure gold; remove a vital working part and the machine will malfunction. What is left is still pure gold -though less of it, but the void has ruined the whole and pervades every aspect. This loss is "evil", and our machine has become a mixture of "gold-and-evil".

Evil is the hole left behind.

Not apples! -Good-and-Evil!

Forget apples! Forget the idiotic innuendo that the forbidden fruit was sex![56] Forget the dreadful misnomer "the tree of knowledge"[57] *No* tree in the Bible is called that *anywhere; there was no such thing,* and it warps the entire message. The real Tree and those counterfeits tradition has snuck in[58] are as unlike as chalk and cheese!

It was:

*"the tree of the knowledge of **good-and-evil**."*

It gave knowledge of a particular **kind** and was called that because the story-teller meant **exactly** what the words say and ***not anything else!***

- Apples from an *apple tree* taste of apple:
- afterwards you know what apples taste of.
- Oranges from an *orange tree* taste of orange
- afterwards you know what oranges taste of.
- "Knowledge fruit" from *a tree of knowledge* would give you a taste of knowledge
- afterwards you would know what you had learned.

- (*Had* there been one it would definitely not have been forbidden anyway! -Knowledge *per se* is consistently positive in the Old Testament.)

• "Knowledge of good-and-evil" fruit

from a *knowledge-of-good-and-evil tree*, will taste good-and-evil.

You will get a first-hand encounter with Evil.

For ever after you will know what Evil *is* and *tastes of*.

Equally important: when you eat fruit, it ends up inside you! For reasons explained later, you will have become what you ate,[59] a mixture of good-and-evil!

Once you've destroyed Perfection you will know what Evil feels like *in practice:* suffering; sickness; cruelty; misery.... Unlike mediaeval folklore, the words used in the Bible indicate:

The Forbidden Tree was the source where you fetched, tasted and experienced and took on board the mix of "good-and-evil".

The reason for forbidding the tree was to spare us from ever tasting the bitter fruit; to prevent us from ruining the functional wholeness of the universe and then having to suffer the consequences that would follow in due course.

* * *

Yet the tree of *the knowledge of good-and-evil* was a *good* tree! It was part of the "very good" God saw on the sixth day of creation. But *this* tree presented a choice to *not* do something[60] and a choice *not* to bring Evil into existence is, of course, a good choice!

So why was it there, anyway? And why else was it "good"? And was it a literal tree or just symbolic?

God is Love, so creatures in God's image need to be Love, too. We were therefore created as Love, which is not only "good", it is "best".

But Love can choose *not* to love. The possibility cannot be prevented, only warned against. So we had the power *not* to love, and the tree was the mirror-image of this capacity. It summarised our capability to stay as Love, or to choose not to love anymore[61]. This is why the tree belonged in the *midst* of the garden and not at the North Pole safely out of harm's way: We could not be separated from what we were; the tree was a reflection of our own hearts!

Whether the tree was a material or symbolic one is immaterial. I leave my readers to decide that for themselves. The results were real enough, so it was real in some sense or other.

Humankind knew "*Good*" already. Right from the start we were surrounded by "*Good*" on every hand. We saw, experienced, tasted and "knew" Good all day and every day, but there *was* no "Evil" to know! Therefore Humankind did not "know good-and-evil" because we cannot know Evil unless it exists.[62]

God can, though. He knows *all* possible states of the universe (including what Evil would be like if it ever came to pass). So God knows "good-and-evil" because He can know Evil *"in theory"*[63] without ever having to make it. Because He knew what Evil would be like, God chose neither to *be* it, nor *make* it![64] Wishing Evil to become a reality would be utterly inconsistent with His Nature.

But Humankind only can know Evil on other terms: Evil has to first *exist in reality* before we can 'know' it. So God never wished Evil on us[65]; never wished Evil to come into being or be visited upon us, never wished Evil to exist for us even in our wildest dreams -What kind of parent wants to give his children nightmares?

Therefore God kept His "Knowledge of good-and-evil" to Himself;

Manufacturing Evil
Vandalism!

- Humankind does not have the power to destroy or detract from God Himself!

- Neither would "Good Humankind" have the inclination to destroy or detract from a perfect creation.

- Nor would "Good Humankind" (normally) have the inclination to destroy or detract from their own perfect nature. The love of God and the love for one another was woven into our being.

- But destruction would be within our power if the choice and self-destruction were the one and same thing.

God is Love, and we were created love, too, because we were in His image. To love God is to keep His commandment.[66] Disobeying Him is therefore also a choice to *not* love God. Now taking the fruit deleted His love within us because it was the *entire process:* choosing, tasting and eating, that destroyed it! The choice and self-destruction were indeed the one and same thing.

Love is a choice and committal, not just a warm fuzzy feeling. As Humankind was created Total Love, choosing to **not** love, violated our nature. No longer were we loving all the way through; The mountain-top had been blasted away, so we became something less.

The power to make completely loving choices now lay forever beyond our scope. From then on, a portion of us was *un*loving. The empty space left by our loss of love was replaced by Egoism. When we were Love, we took the other person as our starting-point. Now that others were no longer our motivation, we only had ourselves left, i.e our "ego". Our ruined self became our resource, not the complete person we had been. The result was that we did things to benefit ourselves, even when it hurt other people or things.[67] The active assertion of egoism upon its surroundings is evil.

So choosing the tree also shut us out of that perfect world of Love. We were excluded from all the choices in the Garden of Eden and turfed out.

Even though a lot stayed good, once our affinity with God was ruined, our egoism began to spread its rot. It permeated every other aspect of our nature and the world around us -even though a lot stayed good. The change also altered our awareness. Our *"eyes were opened"*[68] to a range of possibilities we would have never dreamt of in our original state - evil possibilities: of using our talents and abilities to destructive and cruel ends!

So humankind really <u>did</u> *"know good-and-evil"*[69] like God does; but not on anything like the same terms: We vandalised creation and made Evil a reality. Goodness was something we had known and had tasted of all along, but ever since the Fall, all of humanity has been tasting the fruits of Evil as well, suffering Evil's consequences and knowing it through bitter experience!

Good **and** Creator!

God *can,* therefore, be the creator of all things without having made Evil! For, as Augustine has pointed out, Evil was not "created" in the normal sense of the word.[70]

Whenever you make anything, you have made the possibility of it being destroyed. Evil is that negative potential. The potential arises unavoidably whenever something positive is made. Evil is only of God's "creating" in the *latent* sense of bringing about the possibility, not in the sense of creating the reality. And God expressly forbade *us* to turn Evil into a reality, so it's not His fault![71]

If you destroy absolutely everything, all you have left is a void; nothing at all; non-existence. Nothing is there to be good or be evil because these are qualities of existent things. So Evil is a parasite needing Good to feed on. If nothing Good is left at all, Evil has no mountain left to blast to pieces, nothing to disrupt, corrupt, pervert or anything that can be made to suffer (the things that make *Evil* **evil**). We are only left with Absolute Nothingness. Evil is, therefore, *relative* since Evil is the disruption of Good and only can exist in relation to Goodness.

On the other hand, Good does not need Evil in order to be what *it* is. Goodness arises simply by being made; it comes into being through God Himself and reflects His own Goodness.

So Good is an Absolute; for it is a quality of God Himself and

*"He is light, and in Him is **no** darkness at all."*[72]

Love was Our Lord's Meaning[73]
The Proliferation of Happiness[74]

Our universe was intended to be ruled by Love.[75]

This takes beings that love, so you and I were whirled up out of the dust for the job.[76] But Love is an autonomous process: it is self-determined; it comes from within the Lover and is bestowed freely, not by force. Because Love is a choice, Love is in no way a restriction of God but an expression of His Sovereignty.[77] Therefore, where there is Love, there is also a Free Will.

Love of this quality is not of the ordinary kind.[78] It is the love God *is* and made us to be. In *koiné* (New Testament Greek[79] as opposed to Classical Greek) the word for it is *"agápe"* which in Modern Greek has become the everyday word for love. The New Testament refers to love of a particular *quality*, however: unbounded; committed; faithful; issuing from the Lover and the only truly valid motive for actions:

"Love is patient, love is kind, it is not envious. Love does not brag, it is not puffed up. It is not rude, it is not self-serving, it is not easily angered or resentful. It is not glad about injustice, but rejoices in the truth. It bears all things, believes all things, hopes all things, endures all things. Love never ends."[80]

But because Love is willingly bestowed, with it comes with the possibility of *not* Loving. If that happens, Evil will arise in the gap.

God made Humankind for fellowship with Himself. We learn that He walked in the garden in the cool of the day and called out for Adam. To know God is heaven on earth. It is the highest enjoyment and bliss of all:

"This is life eternal:[81] *that they know*[82] *you, the only true God."*

Common ground is needed if you are to know a person and Love is what puts you on the same wavelength as God. For He *is* Love and without love no true fellowship between you and Him is possible. So love is the key to fellowship with God,[83] and without it even Heaven would not be a heaven! God did not create us Love merely for His own satisfaction. Above all, He did it for *ours:* to give us *Himself!*[84]

To put it simply: God created us Love, to make it possible for us to experience Heaven!

*"The chief end of Man is to glorify God and-***enjoy** *Him forever!"*[85]

Westminster Chatechism

The Plight

Thus was I lerid that love was our Lords mening.
And I saw full sekirly, in this and in all,
that ere God made us, He lovid us,
which love was never slakid, no, never shall.

Julian of Norwich

The Mess We're In

Humankind may have stopped loving God, but that does not mean God stopped loving us! It does determine how He can defeat Evil, though. To understand what He has to do, we have to first consider what problems have arisen.

One:

We can **never** repair destroyed love ourselves. Our scope has been limited by the Fall. We lost something; we were diminished beings; the dimension of total agápe-love is missing from our nature. So if God is to fix things, He must do it Himself.

As God alone is the source of all agapé-love, the power to restore it lies with Him alone. But for God to *force* someone to love is a contradiction in terms. Agapé-love is given willingly, so God cannot simply re-impose it: that would violate our integrity and free will and not bring about the genuine article. We must permit Love to be restored to us or the result will not be real love, just a facade.

Two:

Although much about us stayed good, an alteration had happened at our very core, so the cure will have to happen at our very heart.

Three:

Our function in the world around us is out of joint. We no longer are a harmonious element of the natural ecology. We do things (-often without meaning to,[86]) that are out of step with our environment instead of in keeping with it, and our surroundings are not consistently in keeping with us.

A Heart-condition

God looked upon humankind and found that

*"...every inclination of the thoughts of man's **heart** was only evil all the time."*[87]

The fallen heart corrupts the way all the rest of us works. Our original faculties, talents and desires no longer play out the way God originally planned them. Everything we do becomes an inseparable mixture of good-and-evil; our best acts always have a negative side or consequence to them; our worst misdeeds always some positive spin-off.[88]

Humans are still left with a range of choices: stay as good as we can or stoop even lower and degenerate even further (as happened in the time of Noah). So even in a fallen world some things are worse than others. There are morally good decisions to be made and morally evil acts to be tempted by. But *true* goodness lies hopelessly out of reach.

So the Fall alters the human psyche, perception, inter-action, the way of bringing up children, of treating animals and nature, -the list is endless! But above all, of course, it alters our understanding of God. Not a single person functions any more on the level of the totally committed, loving goodness which once gave us our affinity with Him. Nor can we blame God for this (even though we do!)[89] since we are the ones that brought it about.

In Hebrew, "Sin" is a word that can mean "miss the target". Now we *all* miss the target and our best-aimed arrows fall short of the glory of God.[90] As God is of purer eyes than to look upon sin, our relationship with Him is also broken. *"for what fellowship hath righteousness with unrighteousness? and what communion hath light with darkness?"*[91] We have become the helpless victims of our own diminished nature and never will be good enough. We cannot ever hope to reconcile ourselves to God by doing our best: without love our best will never do.

That is not to say that losing agapé-love leaves us incapable of any love at all, but unable to love in the way God does. So other forms remain and are good: Things like self-love and self-preservation, love of man for woman, woman for man, of mother for child, father for offspring and our love for animals. These are legitimate in themselves and remain, but agape-love was the fail-safe. It was a co-ordinating foundation that welded these loves into intrinsically *positive* forces and now it is gone. Now those loves – Affection – Friendship – Romance, can be warped into unhealthy parodies.92

Humans are only able to pass on to their children what they themselves are.93 So we reproduce variations of an impaired and egoistic humanity. What is more, the offspring of "our first parents" are worse off, since the descendants get a worse starting point: The people raising them are impaired and egoistic and unable to bring up children optimally. The damage will tend to increase rather than diminish.

This may seem hopelessly pessimistic. Fortunately there is a "but":

*"God, who is rich in mercy, because of His great love with which He loved us, even when we were dead in trespasses, made us alive together with Christ (by grace you have been saved)"*94

Personal Evil

In the meantime, we have let loose Evil upon the world. It rampages on and continues to wreak havoc on the original ecology of Creation.[95] To understand Evil's workings, we need to consider what it is and how it functions. Then it becomes easier to see why God is doing what He is about it.

We will not try for a dictionary definition of Evil. The reality may extend beyond the power of words. Instead, we can take a leaf out of Paul's book: he does not define Love, he describes it.[96] So we will try to describe rather than define some aspects of Evil.

Evil is a-turning-away-out-of God's loving plan
It arises through the personal choice to act contrary to God's wishes. Evil is in this sense personal: It is rooted in a self-willed state; a lack or loss; a deliberately chosen malfunction. Evil is therefore an activity (and a state of being as well) that is precisely what God did *not* intend to happen or exist; A state of the universe God chose *not* to create.[97]

Evil is meaningless.

"Meaning" can no more be found in Evil than the sun be found in a sewer. God's creation was positive, purposeful and meaningful: a proliferation of happiness. Because Evil intentionally[98] turns away out of this loving plan of God's, Evil chooses the meaningless instead of the meaningful.

Evil can be personal when *people* are the direct cause of it.

Some evil acts are deliberately performed out of egoism even though the people doing them know what harm they are inflicting -or even because of it. The intention of revenge or terrorism, for example, is to hurt. Furthermore, some acts of evil are predatory: the weak become the target of the strong precisely because they can't hit back.[99] The weak in their turn may take it out on the yet more defenceless.

Personal evil can become even worse still:
It is always easier to go down a mountain than climb up. Some get the deluded idea that Evil is the only meaningful achievement within their scope. They suppose it is the only way they can be successful or achieve fame. (But in reality, Evil is *preventing* them from becoming who they truly are!) Consciously, or through self-deception,[100] a committal to Evil ends up as a choice to place yourself outside the benefits of God's Love -and stay there!

If we fall deeper still, and make a virtue of our own worst traits and greatest weaknesses.[101] we end up finding our life-purpose in wrong-doing and believe our misdeeds define us.[102] Then we draw our pleasures from Evil: The liar despises the unwary who fall for their deceit; the swindler relishes shape-shifting and the power to milk their victims; the scoffer parasitically bolsters up their self-respect by belittling others; the violent get an adrenaline rush from inflicting pain; the sex-predators play their favourite trick and plant the lie: "you really *wanted* it to happen".

In the long run, when a person cannot be dissuaded from the evil they set themselves to do, God may abandon them to their choice.[103] They have *"hardened their heart"* and cannot be dissuaded. So God goes along with it; For example:

Jesus has just washed Judas' feet; Shocking! Now he goes as far as to dip his bread in in the communal dinner dish and shares it with the very man who has set his heart on betrayal. Everyone there knew what was it meant: Only the humblest servant should wash feet! And bread should only be shared with your best friend. But Judas rejects the peace-overtures, and sticks firmly to his treachery; the die is cast. So Jesus says "What you are about to do, do quickly."[104]

But:

1) *Evil is not an absolute, it is a parasite*
   that cannot exist without some degree of goodness to function in,

   and

2) God is still in control.

God remains in control in more senses than one; Firstly: now that Evil has materialised, He works within the parameters of it until He has finished it off for ever.

Secondly:

He is the creator of all things and only in this sense can anyone claim He created Evil: God created the potential for its existence. He did not bring about its reality.

Evil does *not* come from an equal and opposing divinity. The Lord is the origin of the positive thing, and thereby its absence: "I form the light and create darkness; I make peace and create evil: I the LORD do all these things."[105] Darkness is the absence of light; Evil is the absence of good.

Therefore, wherever there is Evil there is a duality -two sides to what goes on. Personal Evil truly *is* a wicked committal, not just an illusion, and it warps goodness; but God can deflect its workings to His own aims. Even though Evil fights against Him, God makes it His unwitting tool!

Thirdly:

> In the same way a pilot is not deflected from his destination
>> nation
> when struggling with the controls of an aircraft in a
>> storm
> Evil cannot turn the Almighty from His purpose
> even though not every twist and turn of the "aeroplane"
>> plane"
> is of His planning.[106]

Fourthly:

> Like a chess-player outsmarting his opponent,
> God outsmarts Evil by exploiting
> the very acts that defy Him most.

Those who know the game of chess will understand how: The true Grand Master has not only a winning strategy but the most threatening moves of the opponent are the very ones the Grand Master exploits to bring victory, so:

"The kings of the earth stood up,
And the rulers were gathered together against the Lord,
And against his Christ...
...For to do
-Whatsoever thy hand and thy counsel determined
before to be done!"
Psalm 2,2 [107]

The opposition to God is real, and the evil is not a mere facade; His enemies do their worst and if the *"princes of this world"* had understood what they were achieving *"they would not have crucified the Lord of glory"*.[108] However, using the very deeds meant to do their worst to Him, God did His Best, deflecting and foiling the works of Evil to defeat it utterly.

* * *

Our suffering has a dual nature, too:

On the one hand is the ill-will behind the evil befalling us and on the other hand the overruling determination of God to turn that evil to our best.

The treatment we get at the hands of Evil brings no comfort with it. You can never hope to understand the "why" of Evil, because it is pointless. There is nothing to be understood. The evil we suffer is perverted and warped and has no further purpose than sadistical gloating enjoyment of our suffering. The woe betiding us is solely intended for our harm and makes no real sense because Evil is rooted in a meaningless choice.

But on God's part there is a plan that is truly good even though its full purpose lies beyond our ken. Many who suffer, claim to having suffered at the hands of God; But if they have, as with Job it is ultimately to the benefit *"of them that are exercised thereby."*[109]

Impersonal Evil

Evil may also be impersonal,
which is another aspect of its dual nature.

Nature is the environment God created not for us alone but all living creatures. Often, we experience nature as a blessing, other times as evil; but in itself it is neither. It is simply impersonal and extremely dangerous if you are in the wrong place at the wrong time.

Once, our open communication with God would have prevented that from happening. Wise before the events, we would have been spectators to firework-displays and grand happenings that in our fallen world cost many lives. But these phenomena are in themselves a by-product of a complex world that did not stop functioning just because we did.

God would have to restructure the universe if He were to prevent so-called natural disasters entirely, for our local phenomena happen in a much bigger context than just planet earth. Who knows what advanced civilisations and perfect creations on other planets might suffer if He did? Nor do we know what local emergency plans are in fact in place to hinder things from getting much worse than they are.

Evil is a random negative consequence of an action and wreaks pointless suffering.

The blows of Evil fall randomly, indiscriminately and the suffering is unfairly and unevenly distributed - particularly wherever Satan and his allies get to put their oar in!. Some people seem to go scot-free while others have a cup brimming with misery. So though many of our troubles are self-inflicted, a great many more are not.

On the other hand, we bring much evil on our own heads without meaning to. Thoughts, words and deeds can have undreamt of results because our understanding is incomplete. They were not meant to harm others, nor willed by anyone in particular but follow of themselves, affecting one-and-all at random. Often they work cumulatively: One negative consequence piles up on the next and sets off an avalanche of tribulations. In economic systems,[110] for example, we may see great personal suffering generated by minor actors struggling in the lights of their limited horizon.

So individual actions may become a cumulative imper-sonal force that -like everything else we do- generates a mixture of good-and-evil.[111]

Finally, the most ugly trait of all:

The prime victims of Evil are the innocent.

The harvest of misery is reaped by those who did not sow it!

- Animals suffer at the hands of cruel task-masters;

- Slaves groan under their despicable slave-drivers;

- Good citizens grieve at the hands of criminals;

- Subjects are crushed by self-seeking authorities;

- Workers are wronged by callous employers;

- Inoffensive school-kids are intimidated by sadistic bul-lies;

- Children wilt at the hands of vindictive or indifferent parents;

- The unborn die at the hands of the abortionist;

"Oh, yes; its always the innocent who suffer"
As the Devil said,
when his mother thrashed him
Because his father had come home drunk!"[112]

Henrik Ibsen

Satan & Co.
-Where do they come in?
If there can be life on other planets,
surely there can be life on other planes of existence,
too?

Granted that our material world is not the only dimension and that other sentient beings exist, then other beings also may be created in the image of God.[113]

We get a hint of this possibility in the rather mystical reference to "the sons of God" that present themselves before the Lord in the Book of Job.[114] These "sons of God" in Job are also portrayed as witnessing the creation of our universe, for God asks:

> *"Where were you when I laid the foundations of the earth?*
> *Tell, if you have understanding...*
> *...When the morning stars sang together,*
> *And all the **sons of God** shouted for joy."*[115]

Satan: the "one who withstands" presents himself among the merry throng though it is not entirely clear whether this adversary is one of these "sons" and what his role is.

We discover that Satan denies there is such a thing as genuine love for God, and we find him to be an agent of calamity who exploits human marauders, natural catastrophes and sickness as tools for his ends.

The fall of humankind helps us understand the origin of the Devil: If *we* can fall by rejecting our innate love, the Devil can, too. That is why we do not need an explanation of his origin: Satan became a devil the same way we became fallen creatures, only earlier on.

This may seem unlikely. Surely beings that were overjoyed when they saw God creating the universe, creatures that have the kind of direct contact with the Lord we read about in Job -surely they would never fall or be fooled into denying their Maker? Yet this need not be as unreasonable as it sounds.

Creation happens in Time and has duration. Until the eyes and brains have been formed, a rational being will not possess the equipment to see or the faculties to grasp what is happening to it. Therefore, even the angels are not able to witness their own making until they wake up somewhere in the middle of the process; And when God says He created them, they have to take His word for it.

So it is feasible for an angel -on gaining consciousness and finding itself a completed being, to refuse to accept it was God's doing. From the angel's viewpoint, all *it* saw was God finishing off something started before it had eyes. So even an angel has to take God's "I made you" on faith! Thus it is logically possible (though totally unreasonable), for a created being to doubt God and to claim it was a product of pre-existent forces: "God has simply finished off and refined a process that started without His intervention".

If Joseph Smith Junior,[116] and Phillip Pullman (in his trilogy "His Dark Materials"[117]) can say such a thing, so can fallen angels; especially when they have a vested interest in saying it. If human beings can be that overweening and presumptuous, and deny their God and Creator, angelic beings can too.

A parallel may be found in Genesis where it describes the creation of the material world. *"God said: "Let there be light", and there was light".* But how do you prove that it was the <u>command</u> that made the light happen? Could it not just be a co-incidence? The connection itself is invisible, it can only be noted, not proven; As the author of Hebrews tells us:

"The things which are seen

*were **not** made of things which are visible."*[118]

In short: the *event* of creation is observable but the *personal input* causing it is not. If someone wishes to assert that the command of God, and the universe coming into existence "just happened to occur at the same moment" and were not connected, then -by a long stretch of the imagination- it is possible. They can claim it was only due to luck, even though that's unreasonable.

But as all Absolutes and Values stem from God, in the final instance their very existence is also an indirect proof that He is indeed the origin of all things. For this reason a devil will be opposed to all Absolutes and will wish to replace them with falsehood (anything will do -so as long as it is not from God[119]). A devil will strive to displace Absolute Truth with "The Relative Standard of Truth"[120] claiming "there are no absolutes".

* * *

Children remind us of their parents. Humankind is a constant reminder of God's reality (being, as we are, in the image of God). We are painful evidence of the existence of God's Authority. We are a visible assertion of the Almighty and His Absolute Standards.

A Satan *"Stir'd up with Envy and Revenge,"* will loathe the very sight of us! A devil will long to destroy us and delight in warping us into his own reflection. Each fall will be a reiteration of Satan's own mutiny and seem to confirm the validity of his rebellion through a bizarre "safety in numbers". That way, our corruption will become part of a larger, more cosmic war between Good and Evil.

The classical explanation of Satan is that he once was an angel but chose to rebel against the Almighty and was cast down from heaven

"what time his Pride
Had cast him out from Heav'n, with all his Host
Of Rebel Angels, by whose aid aspiring
To set himself in Glory above his Peers,
He trusted to have equal'd the most High,
If he oppos'd
(Paradise Lost). Further on we read:

"he above the rest
In shape and gesture proudly eminent
Stood like a Tow'r; his form had yet not lost
All her Original brightness, nor appear'd
Less then Arch Angel ruin'd, and th' excess
Of Glory obscur'd: As when the Sun new ris'n
Looks through the Horizontal misty Air
Shorn of his Beams, or from behind the Moon
In dim_Eclipse disastrous twilight sheds
On half the Nations"
John Milton, "Paradise Lost"[121]

The interesting thing here is that Satan is diminished as a being, but has still many of his original merits and qualities. Following the model of the Fall outlined above, it is not what he has *retained* but what he has *lost*, that makes him the "foul fiend".

The path to an archangel's fall will be different from a human's, but the principle will be the same: Rejecting your Creator means rejecting your love for Him and turning into something else.

An angel who rejects the Creator becomes a fallen angel, even though restoration is possible. But an angel who devotes itself to its fallen nature becomes a devil!

So, did God create the Devil?

Yes, - but not *as* a devil!

Cut off from Life

Death is not in itself evil, it is neutral.[122] Death is a mere consequence of the fact that created things exist within the framework of Time.

All in the realm of Time is transient and temporal[123] - or perpetual at best[124]. Length of life, however, is not the essential point. Some creatures have a cycle of life and death that is very brief -the Mayfly being one of them[125] but its existence is totally valid within its ecological context. The fact something lasts for a little while only does not make it meaningless, just as a song can be lovely but short.

No doubt humankind could see this happening in the world around them.[126] It would be pointless to warn: *"in the day you eat of it you shall surely die"* unless we had a concept of death, and Genesis seems to assume that we did not find the sanction meaningless.

However, humans are beings intended for perpetuity: they had access to a Tree of Life (a source of continual existence). We are told very little about it except that it is one of the good trees we had free access to. Its fruits are clearly food of a different order than our normal intake. It hints that humans were not originally meant to die but live on and on. But they would continually be dependent on an input coming from *outside* themselves.[127]

Only God has life in Himself and all life flows from Him. Anything cut off from God, is therefore cut off from Life. Driven from the Garden and also the Tree of Life our sustenance is gone and *"dying we die."*[128]

A spirit-being exiled from Life, will likewise need sustenance to maintain itself. One way to get it could be by becoming a parasite or predator, sucking on the life of others. Maybe we have an enemy finds in us the tasty morsel he is looking for?

So *"be sober, be vigilant; because your adversary the devil walks about like a roaring lion, seeking whom he may devour."*[129]

The Remedy

"And in this love He hath don all his werks,
and in this love He hath made all things
profitable to us.
And in this love our life is everlestand.
In our making we had beginning.
But the love wherin He made us
was in Him from withoute begynning,
in which love we have our beginning.[130]

If the origin of all things is personal, then the key to understanding our universe lies in the logic of personal relationships[131]. So we need to consider the person of God.

He is the only being in existence that is truly self-determining, for God has no other restriction or limitation except Himself alone.[132] His choice and committal is to be Love -unlimited goodness and more: totally bent on sharing all He Is with us -not because He must, but because He wishes the very best for us.[133]

Genuine Love rises up in defence like "*a she-bear robbed of her cubs*"[134]. Its wrath is kindled against anything hurting the ones it loves because *Evil is the negation of Love* and destroys us "the cubs of God". Therefore, God remains the implacable enemy of *all* Evil and His wrath is eternally kindled against it. God cannot *but* hate and destroy Evil! *Hatred of Evil* is an aspect of true Love! Otherwise Love is no longer the genuine article but sentimentality

But we ourselves have become interwoven good-and-evil, hateful to behold, a blot on His handiwork, and an affront to God's nature. So you and I are -at the one and same time- the objects of His Infinite Love *and* objects of His Total Enmity! -What can He do?

What Can He do?

If the Almighty has the power to stop Evil but does not, this becomes tantamount to God creating Evil by proxy. For the Lord to tolerate wrong is therefore out of the question. It would be the same as agreeing to or acquiescing in Evil's existence, and by the same token make God complicit in all the pain and suffering that unavoidably follows![135]

This leaves certain possible responses,[136] either:

- Destroy Evil and start again

    Or

- Accept Evil temporarily and:
- Restrain it
- Regulate it
- Create the conditions for repairing the damage,
- But set a deadline.

We will now show how, according to the Bible, this is what God, in fact, has done.

Destroy Evil and start again

Starting over?

The first choice comes with a problem: to *remove* Evil means removing *us* since we have become its source. Good-and-evil runs all the way through us like the lettering in a stick of rock-candy. Yet according to the biblical account *"His steadfast love endures for ever"*[137] God never ceased to love us even though the evil and the good in us cannot be separated from each other.[138] So if He must destroy us and start over God will only do it when we get to the point where rescue is impossible: Reform has no foothold any more because our thoughts are set on *"evil only continually"*[139].

It lies completely within God's scope to obliterate humankind, of course, but according to Genesis, He only intervened when restoration no longer had a starting-point. He gave fair warning, set a time limit, and finally had to wipe life out through a flood.[140] Then God began over again with the only person who *did* give Him an opening (i.e. who was prepared to believe Him).

Although God can rid Himself of us and create replacements at any time, He strives not to. His intolerance of Evil is counterbalanced by another principle: grace, undeserved mercy. We read that Noah "found favour" (grace) in the eyes of the Lord. It is not that he was a good man (-Noah was far from perfect we later discover,) but he was willing to *believe* God, act on what he was told and build the Ark.

According to Genesis, we exist today because God had mercy on Noah (and his wife, too[141]). We are all children of Noah so in this sense **all** of us are

"children of grace"

Restrain Evil

Till the End of Time God determined to never again destroy life on earth with a flood and He withdrew the curse upon it.[142] Grace triumphed over annihilation, Evil was curtailed -but not removed, so it has to be restrained.

Restraining Evil is ultimately a pragmatic response conducted on several levels: self-maintenance, hidden restraints, and norms.

Firstly, to some degree Creation is designed to repair itself. Different factors work together to keep things in good shape. For example, we have an autoimmune system protecting us from disease. We also have pain, which is an early warning system to help material beings avoid destructive situations. For this reason, pain is not in itself a "bad" thing[143] even though it is unpleasant (-it wouldn't work if it were nice!).

Secondly, unseen hidden restraints are hinted at. We read *"my Spirit shall not strive with man forever"*. This indicates that on God's part there may be a continued action going on within our hearts: In a much later book we learn: *"For the secret power of lawlessness is already at work; but the one who now holds it back will continue to do so till he is taken out of the way."*[144] This suggests that a continued "something" is holding back Evil and making wrongdoing have other effects than the forces of Evil intended; but one day the hindrances will be taken away and, as the saying goes, "all Hell will be let loose"[145].

Thirdly, the tendency of humans to live, act and work collectively in societies leads to the need for common norms -keeping our appointments, for example. These norms tend to help maintain a certain functional minimum. So governments and authorities are designed to be God's servants i.e. they are agents with a role to fulfil and when they conform to the purpose of their Grand Commissioner, they limit the effects of Evil.[146]

Regulate Evil: God's three-fold strategy

- Wisdom
- God's Law
- Conscience

Tempt a bird with a plate of delicious worms and you may very well succeed; Tempt a human on the other hand and you will not be likely to find many takers.

> *"When the woman saw that the fruit of the tree was good for food and pleasing to the eye, and also desirable for gaining wisdom, she took some and ate it."*[147]

There are positive desires innate to our nature implied in the Creation Story, reason being one of them. Eve can only be tempted by something she already finds attractive: food, love of beauty and the desire for wisdom. So the serpent, when he argues with her, exploits woman's power of reasoning, love of beauty and desire for wisdom and her wish to contribute something positive to her husband.

Scripture explains how our faculties were used as weapons against our Love but does not imply that they are negative in themselves or lost to us.[148] So God makes use of the common ground between us to restrict Evil even though communication with Him has been hampered by the Fall.

• Wisdom

God may work by appealing to our desire to attain wisdom. Wisdom appeals to reason and knowledge but goes beyond them: it is "the right way to use knowledge". In other words, it is not so much a case of "what you know" as of "how to apply what you know in a positive and practical way."

Very simple and humble people may shine with wisdom and very learned and educated people are sometimes utter fools. Wisdom is not the prerogative of the few or learnéd and it is found in every society and all walks of life.

Wisdom is portrayed in the Bible as a free meal everyone is invited to; a free gift from God. The only price is having enough self-knowledge to admit you need wisdom:

*"(Wisdom) says to those **who lack judgement**.*

*Let all who are **simple** come in here!"*[149]

Rightly applied wisdom hinders Evil and promotes peaceful relations. It has universal appeal and you do not have to belong to a particular religion or agree with a particular philosophy to find it helpful.

• God's Law

Reason is a second common ground that God appeals to.

God recommends principles for our good and rules to restrict Evil, e.g. the Law of Moses (the Torah) found in Exodus.[150] A rational person can easily see how following the Law is enlightened self-interest. *"Loving your neighbour as yourself"*[151] -which is the sum of the Law- would benefit me and everyone else, too.

But the society the Torah regulates is one where bad things happen and crimes are committed: husbands get jealous of their wives, people hit each other, or develop skin diseases, among other things. The Torah prescribes remedies -but this is not the same as saying that sticking to it will bring the world God wishes for. For example, the Law lays down rules for divorce -and yet we learn that God hates divorce![152]

In short, the Torah is a pragmatic answer to the way people truly are, not a description of how ideal people behave. But if the Law were obeyed it would bring us closer to the ideal, provide a modicum of healthy social conditions and transform society;[153] you would never need to lock your door anymore! Law is not a perfect tool[154] but it can restrict Evil and limit the increase of destruction and suffering.

Our motives for following the Law will rest on several pillars. These will include sanctions, social pressures and internalised values. The sanctions and social pressures will exert control externally, and give us codes of conduct. Our internalised values will influence us via our conscience as well as our habits and priorities.

• Conscience

Any creature with the innate power of choice has a debate going on inside on what to choose. Knowing good-and-evil has changed the discussion from "which of two *equally good* things do I choose" (mangoes or bananas?) to

- "will this decision produce *good or bad* results?"

- "Should I choose results that are not good for me now but might be good in the future or might be bad for me now but good for someone else?" – And so on and so forth.[155]

Ethical decisions have to be made and wrong choices normally leave the person at best uncomfortable and at worst tortured. We call this inner judge "the conscience"[156] and it is one of the ways God stays in touch with us.

Neither unaided wisdom nor reason produce good results unfailingly and both can be perverted. The conscience, however, is a meeting point between our reason and emotions and has the power to act as a corrective when the other two go astray.

Our conscience is not infallible, and may build on misconceptions; But on the other hand, people who lack a conscience (or maybe deliberately ignored it,) may also lack the inner controls hindering them from self-destructive acts. They often end up socially isolated, miserable and outcasts. Conscience may exert its power subjectively but let that not fool us to think it less real or valid.

* * *

Armed then, with the triple resources of Wisdom, Law and Conscience, the individual will have a good foundation for making choices that promote good and avoid evil.

Before the Fall we were functioning agents of the goodness of God. We were one of the channels through which He worked and materialised His blessings. We can still be His agents for at least *some* of the time. If we follow God's ways we can make a real difference to those people we do good to. We in our turn reap the benefits of other people's good works. More than this: we then also live out a portion of our original dignity and worth, even though it be marred and incomplete.

However, our standing with God is not decided by how well we behave, though our fellowship is! Without agapé-love we all fall short anyway so we are always dependant on our status as *"Children of Grace"*.

The remedies described above are only temporary checks to Evil -stop-gaps, not fail-safes. The true answer is to repair the damage, restore us and remove Evil that way. But the consequences of Evil are very real, so they have to be dealt with through concrete practical intervention. Although wisdom, law and conscience curtail Evil, it is not removed; its scope may be dampened, but it is not dissolved.

God still cannot root out Evil without destroying me and you; And He loves us! -What is He to do?

Repair the Damage

Evil has very real consequences -For us!
So God took the consequences upon Himself -
To spare us!

Tolerating the Intolerable,[157] God "took it like a man". He became human in the person of Jesus.[158] To reconcile His love for us and His hatred of Evil, God has done everything it takes. This does not mean that He stopped functioning as God, but He, in Jesus, took on His self-portrait and showed us His nature by becoming fully human and living on exactly the same terms as anyone else.

However, because He was still that Love all humankind *should* have been had they never fallen, Jesus was without sin. So Jesus is the expression of who God Is: *The* Word that expresses and spells out though flesh and blood the "I AM" i.e. God's own self-summary.

A true man shoulders responsibility; the buck stops here. So God in the person of Jesus, shouldered the responsibility of rectifying the wrong.[159] Even though He was not the guilty party, God interposed His body and warded off the deadly lashes of our Fall. He let every concrete result of Evil: every sorrow, every suffering, every grief, be vented upon Himself instead of humankind, not because He wished to, but because we needed Him to. In Jesus, He shouldered the Cross and put Himself between us and the fruit of our actions because only *God* is great enough to take on the out-workings of Evil and neutralise the blows!

Suffering and Death therefore happened to God personally instead of you and I. The results of our wickedness fell upon Him instead of us. Hanging upon the Cross, Jesus shielded us from our obliteration. He reaped the harvest of Evil we had sown, and paid the price. And because He was fully human, Jesus could also represent us and pay for all humankind.

"Concentrated in a span of space and time", in the Cross we see also what Evil costs God subjectively. For every evil act wrenches God's heart and feels like living torture. He has to put up with us and tolerate the intolerable instead of blotting us out.[160] He sees and empathises totally with the misery of all, whether innocent or guilty, deserving or not. God knows the suffering that follows implacably wherever Evil holds sway, and He yearns to put an end to it. Actively and constantly He works against it. But before He can obliterate Evil, God must bide His time. He must wait, for there are still people He can salvage from this titanic shipwreck.

What has to be bourn in mind is that though death on the Cross was a matter of hours, God's suffering was *outside* of time and vast and unimaginable in extent.[161] This is why His sacrifice was absolutely adequate and has the power to cover the guilt not of just *one* person, but of an entire world![162] Once done, *"it is finished!"*[163]

Evil is the negation of everything God *is;* What God did in Christ was take this total negation upon Himself. He who knew no Sin, became Sin. Yet taking Sin in upon Himself spelt death to His own nature! Therefore He called out as the darkness surrounded Him *"My God, my God, why have you forsaken me?"*

But:

God is absolute, Evil is not.

"the light shines in the darkness, and the darkness could not swallow it up".[164]

God is greater and mightier than the very worst Evil can muster against Him.

So death itself could not defeat Him:

The third day He rose from the dead!

Endgame

In one fell swoop our Grand Master gained the upper

hand. The endgame has begun and things are moving on towards that final "checkmate".

What did His action achieve? Much that is beyond our ken -for who can fathom the plans of one whose I.Q. is Infinity Plus?[165] But we *do* grasp some things.

First: the perfectly justifiable fury that God felt at the ruination of His wonderful act of creation: His paradise turned into misery; His children turned vicious; all this anger God vented upon Himself, choosing to turn His wrath in upon Himself and take the blame rather than blame us; For it is always the forgiver that pays the price.

Second: He took Evil upon His own shoulders; He who knew no Sin became embodied Sin and Evil received its unavoidable consequence: Death (for God is absolutely *not* going to put up with Evil for ever). In this manner

God atoned for our Sin. Justice was done and *seen* to be done.

This way God is fair. Intolerant of Evil as He *should* and *must* be, He forgives Evil while neither ignoring nor condoning it by paying for it Himself. So He is within His rights when He condemns, but Just when He forgives.

Third: God swallowed in the sea of His Mercy all the negative consequences flowing from our Fall. He descended into the venomous environment of Good-and-Evil and endured the unendurable and absorbed the unacceptable.

Yet absorbing Evil could not poison God or make Him bad; Figuratively speaking, He became "even better" - He became our Saviour! Not that God changed really, but what was true about Him from the beginning was now visible. He showed that He was a "redeemer"[166] -someone who buys his relatives back from slavery.

Fourthly: *"Love is as strong as death"* Swallowing that bitter pill *"death was swallowed up in victory"*[167] and Death could not contain Him.

Like an atom-bomb within an egg,

exploding out,

Life was victorious, Jesus rose again!

And doing so He disintegrated Death for ever.

Reconciliation
Yet this was only the beginning.

Jesus is therefore alive right now: If He rose again then He is not dead!

Risen from the dead He comes into our hearts to be Himself and live there. God the Holy Spirit is ready to move in, plant His own life within us and restore the agapé-love we lost at the Fall.

So radical is the effect that it can only be described as a total renewal. We are new creatures -for nothing can ever be the same once God has entered our very core and His sufficiency fills the void. We are not merely able to love God the way we were at the beginning

*"God has poured out his love into our hearts by
the Holy Spirit, whom he has given us."*[168]

He Himself supplies the love we once were created to be, and we consent to Him and become loving beings. Since it is *His* life come to life in us, this makes us His children, born from above.[169]   Just as the loss of our agapé-love pervaded all the rest, (-good though the rest had been) so the restoration of that love pervades all the rest of us (-corrupted though the rest has become).[170]

No longer are we "good-and-evil" but "good-and-better" because His resurrection-life pervades our lives; but this is only the case as we hold ourselves close to God and "abide in Him"[171]. Apart from Him we are exactly what we were before: helpless sinners![172] So with Christ dwelling within our hearts, evil is destroyed from within and we are perfected.

"Therefore, if anyone is in Christ, he is a new creation; the old has gone, the new has come!"

Aorist Passive Subjunctive

Therefore, you, dear reader, are going to have to decide whether or not to let God fix you!

When Jesus talked to Nicodemus of being "born anew" he used the Greek tense "aorist passive subjunctive".

- Aorist means the action happens *there and then*, not slowly over time.

- Passive means it *is done to* you, you do not do it yourself.

- Subjunctive means it is dependent on *conditions*.[173]

When you encounter truth from God, you recognise it as truth *there and then*.[174]   The recognition draws forth faith in you just as a magnet induces magnetism in iron that was not magnetic before. So the faith comes from God, not you.[175]

Accept! These are the *conditions*: It may feel to you like something *you* do, and in a sense it *is* -you make a response; but objectively it is God drawing it forth and you don't hinder it. Don't draw back and reject faith when it rises within.

God is generous and understands the meaning of your heart so *any* genuine response will do, really. However, if you need the help: Jesus wants to take up dwelling within you so talk to Him, He can hear you![176] Tell Him you believe He *did* rise from the dead and *is* alive today and ask Him to forgive your wrong-doing and come into your heart. Then afterwards, thank Him for keeping His promise.

"If you declare with your mouth that Jesus is Lord, and believe in your heart that God raised him from the dead, you will be saved."

Because God is generous, He is prepared to give you chance after chance. The offer still stands but every moment your response is delayed, Evil is prolonged; and there is a deadline: Nobody knows when time will run out.

The Abolition of Evil

"The reason the Son of God appeared was to destroy the works of the devil." 177

The Abolition of Evil is a complicated process worked out over time, painfully and painstakingly. But the practical destruction of Evil begins from the moment Christ enters our heart. In the course of time this renews of all our habits, thoughts, attitudes and relationships, (-as long as we don't put the brakes on). Old destructive ways have to be broken. Evil longings have to be turned away from. Much has to be healed, much has to be unlearned and still more yet needs to be re-learned. For, as we saw earlier, the works of God are dynamic, progressing from glory to glory.

During the learning process we have now entered into, our natural talents and abilities are restored to their rightful place. The tide of Evil is turned back. Everything we *are* is reclaimed from destructive ends and restored to its original intended role.

All the same, our true resource is always Christ Himself, therefore our relationship with Him is paramount. Jesus is like the fuel in a car: without gasoline the car will not go; without Jesus no one can live the Christian life. Like Samson shorn of his hair,[178] shorn of Christ and cut off from the source of our strength we *become as weak as any other man.*"

Once God has reconciled us, we are restored to that fellowship we were supposed to have with Him from the beginning. Our original dignity and worth returns. We have a part to play as God continues the work of defeating Evil by bringing more people "soul by soul" into a relationship with His Son; From now on we can be agents of God's love to the world around us *"because as He is, so are we in this world"*. But this is only a foretaste of what God has in store. Go "further up and further in". Everyone is invited.

In the meantime the world is still at an interim stage. Many have not yet encountered God's truth. Many have rejected His truth and turned to other devices. Evil is still revoltingly active, therefore, and its defeat is an on-going affair. The forces of Evil have no intention of rolling over and dying. They continue to fight by foul means -as often as possible, and fair -if they absolutely must.

But the Bible ends with this promise:

The Kingdom of Heaven shall come to earth.

Evil *shall* be destroyed for ever!

Solving the Problem of Evil

The Bible *does* therefore provide an intellectually comprehensible and cohesive answer to the old problem

"How can God be Almighty,

Good and Creator of all things,

in a world so patently evil?"

It is our proposition that the explanation is outlined in principal in the first 800 words of the Bible, followed through in the subsequent parts and completed in the last! This is its answer:

God is Love
He made a Perfect universe with no Evil in it
Evil arises in the gap if you rip a hole in Perfection.
If you do, the rest stays good
so you end up with a mix of good-and-evil.

We were part of that perfection and created loving beings
so we could enjoy Him, -which is the same thing as Heaven,
for without fellowship with God, even Heaven would not be a heaven.

The source of good-and-evil was forbidden us

But the possibility of choosing it could not be kept from us

because we were Love, like God is, and Love is a choice,

so the choice lay within our own frame.

We chose not to Love,
And this lovelessness was that gap that created Evil
We were now good-and-evil ourselves.
So God has to plug the hole to fix things.

Therefore He has bandaged us by giving us

Wisdom, Law and Conscience, to slow the bleeding

and God has let the consequences of Evil happen to Himself instead of us!

This He did through coming as Jesus Christ and dying on the cross.

He is now healing that hole

by filling our hearts with His own love through the Holy Spirit

wherever souls accept Him.

Finally He will intervene and destroy Evil for ever.

But Humankind does not *really* need to understand why Evil exists,

-What *we* need **is to be *rid* of it!**

That is why God's answer does not rest solely on an appeal to the intellect. The solution He has given us is pragmatic, intellectual and *personal* -a person:

Jesus Christ

Acknowledgments

Thanks to all who have encouraged me on the way: S. K. who proof-read the appalling Norwegian of my first outline ("Trenger Gud Briller") and Arve Brunvoll (systematic theologian and then director at NLA) who read it with an open mind. His comment (on my Norwegian,) was: "Høyst sjarmerende språkbruk" (highly charming language use) and on the contents: "you have not solved the problem but placed it somewhere it is not usually thought of being". My answer was: "That sounds right, because the mystery is then in the nature of Love, which seems more like where any mystery should belong."

Thanks also to those who have been willing to plough through the later (English) versions and give them their consideration, including Oddbjørn Aasen, and Judith Irene Dahl who also kick-started me into weeding out all the typos and punctuation errors. Thanks also to Joanna Penn, of theCreativePenn.com whose online advice and directions got me moving in the right direction, and Jens Jakob Jensen, of Tema Design and filemon.no whose help with the layout and cover-design have lifted the whole quality of the result.

Thank you Megan Easley Walsh (meganeasleywalsh.com) my editor who has contributed invaluable comments and insights and helped me bring my book on to where it is. Her services are recommended!

Last but not least: thank you, BFJ, who first spurred me to put pen to paper.

* * *

My sins are very original: they are all my own work. Any errors[179], inclarities and dodgy theology must be laid to my account.

Richard Mure Exelby, Bergen, Norway, March 2018

Frontispiece: Spomenik na Sajmištu Pinki at Serbian Wikipedia. Public Domain Sajmište Monument on the site of the Nazi Concentration Camp on the banks of the Sava at Belgrade, Serbia, in memory of the estimated 23000 Serbians and Jews who died there. Many Serbians who did not die there were sent on to Jasenovac -a camp notorious for its brutality, where the lowest estimate of deaths is 77000 and the highest anything up to over a million.

Within: [Image: Sumerian cuneiform and figures by Fedor Selivanov on shutterstock.jpg] [Image: Nikkitok - 123RF recomposed by author to: Good-and-Evil - with hole-in-heart_filled with Evil.jpg] Warp and Weft http://commons.wikimedia.org/wiki/ User:Ryj "Brighton Rock"   by lilivanili on Flickr Brighton Rock2729305452_162a1f2254_z (The reference to Graham Greene's novel of the same name is not unintentional.) checkmate-1653310 by Archies7 via Pixabay

Quotes from Julian of Norwich, *Revelations of Divine Love, chapter 86* viaUniversity of Rochester, NY Robbins Library digital projects (TEAMS Middle English Texts series)

Bible quotation sources unless otherwise specified are from the Blue Letter Bible.

NB & Links:

There are many footnotes in this text. If you click on the number of the footnote, an e-book or word-processor will jump there and you can read the footnote if you wish. To return to your place in the book, you must then click on the number of the footnote and then it will leap back again.

Links

1. You matter.
   https://youtu.be/pNYw2RHowGA
2. Womankind, -Creation's Crown.
   https://youtu.be/KKOGZgFJkPE
3. Evil - "How Come?"
   https://youtu.be/mZD1qi5DycQ
4. Evil – "Why did God allow it?"
   https://youtu.be/D5bl2ipCs5U
5. Evil – "What Next?"
   https://youtu.be/GquXnDIA3oY
6. The Atom-bomb and the Egg.
   https://youtu.be/ycIlP445Yus
7. Evil –defeating it forever.
   https://youtu.be/zn9XDQqG94I

About the Author

Richard Mure Exelby Canadian born, British raised, and now resident and citizen of Norway.

He grew up in Hove, Sussex, on the south coast of England, but his grandmother's family came from Orkney so he became interested in the Vikings from an early age. Not unsurprisingly, he read Scandinavian Studies at the University of East Anglia and learned Norwegian there.

An atheist from the age of six, he rejected religion out of hand until something radical happened: according to himself, he had an encounter with God and made the discovery that Jesus did rise from the dead. The upshot was that Exelby moved to Norway, where he followed the same career pattern as the average immigrant: Beginning by doing unskilled labour he later studied, and finally became qualified for other work. In his case he gained recognition for his B.A and added on to it. He could then teach in the Norwegian school system. Subsequently he further qualified as "Lektor" -a teacher with a post-graduate degree of a somewhat higher standing than a Masters.

In the course of his career he has been factory worker at a bakery, general cleaning-assistant, carpet-cleaner, Youth Club leader and teacher at Secondary School and later on at High School. However, his purpose in coming to Norway was to fulfil a calling. From the day he first stepped off the boat in Norway he always considered himself an emissary for the Lord and a servant of the people he was sent to assist, so he has continually worked with that in mind. Among other things he has translated a number of songs into English including a whole musical, and some of them he has uploaded to his YouTube channel. In 1999 his attention and sympathy was directed to Serbia, and he began to take an interest in its welfare. For this reason he is currently learning Serbian - at the break-neck speed of a glacier.

Short Bibliography and web-resources
Printed sources

Lewis C.S "The Last Battle" Bodley Head 1956

Encyclopaedia Britannica. Encyclopaedia Britannica 2009 Ultimate Reference Suite. Chicago

Exelby, Richard Mure: The Deacons' Assignment in the Light of the New Testament Material, Bergen 1997

Fausset, A.R. The First Epistle of Paul the Apostle to the Corinthians

Hasegawa, Tsuyoshi Racing the enemy: Stalin, Truman, and the surrender of Japan p. 240 Harvard 2005

Ibsen, Henrik trans R. Farquharson Sharp Peer Gynt London, Dent - Everyman Series 1956

John Milton, Paradise Lost, London 1674. Book 1

Julian of Norwich, Revelations of Divine Love, (div publishers).

Kierkegaard, Søren Philosophiske Smuler, 1844

Marx, Theses On Feuerbach: Thesis 3 (1845)

Michelsen, Leif M. Fortolkning til Første Mosebok Oslo 1972. Lutherstiftelsens Forlag; Lunde Forlag. ISBN 82 531 0634 8

New American Standard Version (1995)

Jones, Alexander ed. Jerusalem Bible. Darton Longman and Todd, 1966

Pullman, Philip The Amber Spyglass, Scholastic Uk Ltd 2000

The Westminster Shorter Catechism1647

W. Woodruff, T. Bullock, and W. Clayton. Journal of Discourses, Volume 6, pages 1-11. A Discourse, by President Joseph Smith (Joseph Smith Jnr.) Delivered at the Conference held near the Temple, in Nauvoo, April 6, 1844 Reported by W. Richards,

Web links

http://biblicalhebrew.org/hebrew-names-of-god-in-the-bible.aspx

http://biblos.com/genesis/2-17.htm

http://en.wikipedia.org/wiki/Mayfly or http://da.wikipedia.org/wiki/Døgnflue where we are told that many of these only live at the adult stage for a few hours! i.e, created to be ephemeral. Their life-cycle is their form of perpetual life.

http://en.wikipedia.org/wiki/Names_of_God_in_Judaism#The_Tetragrammaton;

http://en.wikipedia.org/wiki/Quantum_leap

http://library.taylor.edu/dotAsset/afcf88aa-52b7-4dda-8e6b-d5efd2e6b1f6.pdf

http://necrometrics.com/pre1700a.htm#20worst

http://www.archive.org/stream/peergyntdramaticooibseuoft/peergyntdramaticooibseuoft_djvu.txt

http://www.biblegateway.com/

http://www.blueletterbible.org/ lexicon.

http://www.blueletterbible.org/Bible.cfm?b=Gen&c=2&v=7&t=NKJV#conc/17

http://www.blueletterbible.org/Bible.cfm?b=Jhn&c=1&v=17&t=KJV#vrsn/5

http://www.blueletterbible.org/Bible.cfm?b=Jhn&c=3&v=5&t=KJV#vrsn/3

http://www.catholic.org/bible/book.php?id=24

http://www.creeds.net/Westminster/shorter_catechism.html

http://www.jstor.org/discover/10.2307/1515709?uid=3738744&uid=2129&uid=2&uid=70&uid=4&sid=47698820306447

http://www.marxists.org/archive/marx/works/subject/quotes/index.htm

http://www.ntgreek.org/learn_nt_greek/subj-detail-frame.htm

http://www.str.org/site/News2?page=NewsArticle&id=5124

http://www.thelutheran.org/article/article.cfm?article_id=5895&key=34751023

http://www.truthandgrace.com/joesinner.html

https://www.blueletterbible.org/kjv/psa/94/9/t_bibles_572009

Endnotes

¹ Marx, <u>Theses On Feuerbach: Thesis 3</u> (1845) "The philosophers have only interpreted the world, in various ways; the point is to change it." http://www.marxists.org/archive/marx/works/subject/quotes/index.htm

² So when He is done they will be obliterated. Re 21:4 *"And God shall wipe away all tears from their eyes; and there shall be no more death, neither sorrow, nor crying, neither shall there be any more pain: for the former things are passed away."*

³ The classical Epicurean objection had been summarised by the philosopher Hume succintly: *"Epicurus's old questions are yet unanswered. Is he willing to prevent evil, but not able? then is he impotent. Is he able, but not willing? then is he malevolent. Is he both able and willing? whence then is evil?"* Dialogues concerning Natural Religion (1779).

<u>But Epicurus' argument rests upon a false hidden presupposition.</u> It assumes that God is doing nothing about Evil. But He most certainly is! It is just that we are still in the middle of things, and Evil is therefore not yet visibly banished from the universe.

The objections *have* been answered. God *is* willing, and prevents evil every day. He *is* able, but using restraint, His *is* omnipotent but holds His destruction in reserve in order not to destroy YOU if He can avoid it. He is able and *has* done what it takes at a cost and through a love that boggles the mind! And evil exists now only under sufferance until there are no more survivors God can salvage from the titanic shipwreck of this world.

So *Epicurus's old objections* boil down to this: "The police have not arrived yet in response to the emergency call, therefore there are none coming." "*I* cannot see how God is preventing evil, so he is not doing it; because the way *I* think he should do it is not happening. The only possible explanation, therefore, is that he is impotent or malevolent -because it is unthinkable that I am short-sighted or uninformed."

⁴ Whether Genesis actually "quotes", "makes use of" or "builds upon other sources", is of course an academic moot point (it seems fairly obvious that it does). It should not mislead us into overlooking what the final product has to say.

5 examples may be found at: http://www.cs.williams.edu/~lindsey/myths/myths.html

6 When Prometheus helped us by giving us fire, he was condemned to eternal punishment for his 'crime'.

7 "I spect I grow'd." Topsy's amused answer in Harriet Beecher Stowe's <u>Uncle Tom's Cabin</u> https://www.gutenberg.org/files/203/203-h/203-h.htm

8 There are really only two possibilities: **either** the original agency of existence is *Impersonal* (as with chaos: non directional and non-planned with any semblance of order being ultimately an illusion,) **or** the agency is *Personal*, (the universe being an intelligent, motivated product; planned even when making use of autonomous or self-directed forces to achieve the aims).

This does not, of course, explain where God Himself comes from. But then again, the existence of *existence itself* cannot be explained in terms of causality ("cause and effect") as it simply ends up in an infinite regress ("What caused the original Cause?").

There is, of course the pseudo-argument that everything goes round in a never-ending ring, having no beginning or end. But this is merely avoiding the issue: The unanswerable question then becomes: "where, then, does the ring as a **whole**, come from?"

How does God create from nothing? maybe by taking a corner of His Infinite might and polarising it into matter and antimatter.

9 Any discussion of "cause and effect" places things within the context of time, because a cause has to happen before the effect. (Thank you, Alexandra Hoines, for pointing this out). However, God did not create *within* time, said the old divines, He created all *together with* time, in other words **time** was created by God. But He himself was not caused. He exists outside of time, and simply IS.

[10] according to current theories. Black holes possibly spew the materials they suck in out into "multiverses" in other dimensions, which then possibly spewed their materials back into ours. So one ends up with the "ring" discussed in the endnote above, and the question remains: where did the multiverses in their entirety come from, then? - or for that matter the quantum loops in their entirety? https://news.nationalgeographic.com/news/2010/04/100409-black-holes-alternate-universe-multiverse-einstein-wormholes/ No doubt in a.d. 2500 this whole discussion will seem naïve.

[11] (Not that I concede Hebrew numerology to be anything more than a literary device, I do not accept that it has magical properties)

[12] i.e, not pronounced good *per se* (Latin: "intrinsically: with respect to its inherent nature"; "this statement is interesting per se" wordnet.princeton.edu/perl/webwn)

This can be taken a number of ways, for example that Humankind was good, that Humankind was amoral, or that humankind would become "good" or "bad" through an existential decision. I consider the first is nearest the truth since everything was good when God beheld the finished world, but the others are also worth consideration.

[13] Many translations and commentators put the phrase at the *end* of the First Creation Story, rounding off the tale. Though the phrase does serve as an elegant bridge between the two, there is more than enough reason to consider it the heading to the second part, with the setting up of Eden and all that happens there. Everywhere else in the Bible the phrase is **without exception** the introduction to the material that follows: a list of ancestors and relations and some of the events in their lives. The expression *never* refers to what went before elsewhere, so there is no reason to treat it any differently here. In Genesis it is found in this form 10 times, once in the form "this is the book of the generations of" and once in Ruth. 12 times all told.

Ge 2:4 These <u>*are*</u> <u>the</u> <u>generations</u> *(birthings)* <u>of</u> the heavens and of the earth when they were created, in the day that the LORD God made the earth and the heavens,

Ge 5:1 Th<u>*is is the book of*</u> the <u>generations</u> of Adam:

Ge 6:9 These <u>*are*</u> <u>the</u> <u>generations</u> <u>of</u> Noah: Noah was a just man *and* perfect in his generations, *and* Noah walked with God.

Ge 10:1 Now <u>these</u> <u>*are*</u> <u>the</u> <u>generations</u> <u>of</u> the sons of Noah, Shem, Ham, and Japheth: and unto them were sons born after the flood.

Ge 11:10 These <u>*are*</u> <u>the</u> <u>generations</u> <u>of</u> Shem: Shem *was* an hundred years old, and begat Arphaxad two years after the flood:

Ge 11:27 Now <u>these</u> <u>*are*</u> <u>the</u> <u>generations</u> <u>of</u> Terah: Terah begat Abram, Nahor, and Haran; and Haran begat Lot.

Ge 25:12 Now <u>these</u> <u>*are*</u> <u>the</u> <u>generations</u> <u>of</u> Ishmael, Abraham's son, whom Hagar the Egyptian, Sarah's handmaid, bare unto Abraham:

Ge 25:19 And <u>these</u> <u>*are*</u> <u>the</u> <u>generations</u> <u>of</u> Isaac, Abraham's son: Abraham begat Isaac:

Ge 36:1 Now <u>these</u> <u>*are*</u> <u>the</u> <u>generations</u> <u>of</u> Esau, who *is* Edom.

Ge 36:9 And <u>these</u> <u>*are*</u> <u>the</u> <u>generations</u> <u>of</u> Esau the father of the Edomites in mount Seir:

Ge 37:2 These <u>*are*</u> <u>the</u> <u>generations</u> <u>of</u> Jacob. Joseph, *being* seventeen years old, was feeding the flock with his brethren; and the lad *was* with the sons of Bilhah, and with the sons of Zilpah, his father's wives: and Joseph brought unto his father their evil report.

[14] "Birthings/Generations" in Hebrew: תּוֹלְדוֹת toledaw. It is a good name for the book laying the premises for the entire Bible.

15 In theological terminology: "lesearten" (reading-genre) of the entire pericope (Chapter 2:4 till chapter 4:26). To ignore the genre of a Bible passage when reading it is as unwise as over-looking the currency symbol on a price tag: £20 is not the same as $20 or as €20!

16 (in short, Genesis chapter 1 **the Chronology**, and Genesis chapter 2 **the Genealogy**)

17 One might ask: Why not simply give us the integrated version straight off? My guess is, is that the job of integration sets off processes within us that make our relationship with God grow. (God as a person, I mean). see next footnote

18 John 5:39 "You study the scriptures, believing that in them you have eternal life; now these same scriptures testify to me, and you refuse to come to me for life! (Jerusalem Bible; London, 1974

19 Genesis 4,2 -Male and female created he them; and blessed them, and called **their** name Adam אָדָם, in the day when they were created.

20 as explained in a lecture on Genesis held by a jewish Rabbi at Akron Ohio ca. 2005.

21 The terminology for the process of creation of the human and animal world is related to the terms used in ceramics. The word "form" ruy yatsar is used of a potter elsewhere in the Bible (Jeremiah 18,3). And we also now know from the study of epigenetics that DNA doesn't just work mechanically. Different genes get triggered or shut down under way, and this brings about variations in the result, for example, poodles get curly hair. There are also things to suggest that taming animals (e.g. selecting the tamer foxes rather than the wild and aggressive ones,) tends to trigger off further changes in their appearance or the colour of their fur, also. Tweaking DNA and pushing and prodding clay are quite similar activities. But you can hardly expect people living 2000 B.C to express themselves in 21st century language, and it's just as well they didn't, because in the 29th century our scientific insights will sound naïve, too.

22 Nor was it taken to when Darwin published his ideas. Huxley is more to blame for *that* controversy. (No doubt I have just made myself a lot of enemies, but "if I try to please people, I am no longer a servant of God" (Galatians 1:10).) The question is not whether God *can* make the entire universe in 144 hours flat -of course He can! -but whether Genesis *actually* says He *did*. 'Day' in Hebrew can mean a period of time.Besides this, although we assume the "days" of Genesis 1 are meant to be taken as happening consecutively, this may be something we have taken for granted where listeners thousands of years ago might not. I would like to remind readers that this text is probably over 4000 years old, so you should be careful how categorical you are about it.

23 Beware of drawing too wide conclusions from God breathing into the man. Exactly the same is said of the animals. It almost certainly only means natural breath, not some spiritual quality. (cf. Ezekiel 37:9 the 4 winds come i.e. physical winds, not the Holy Spirit, and make the dry bones live.)

24 Joh 4:24. "God *is* a Spirit: and they that worship him must worship *him* in spirit and in truth". God is called "Father" because the material universe is something *other* than God, not a continuum of His existence, not "His visible surface" (as in pantheism). Fathers reproduce outside themselves, yet are the origin, while mothers produce from *within* themselves and are the origin. No slight is intended on the ladies, -to call God "Mother" would be to misconstrue or misrepresent the relationship of the creation to the Creator. If God is "mother" this is seen in His Infinite Love and ongoing compassion and concern for our welfare even though these are qualities found in both a mother and father; c.f Isaiah 49:15

25 and just as the dust is nothing in itself, so are we: -significant only because of what we express, not the materials we are composed of. A Ming vase is made of ordinary materials, but the input of the artist makes it priceless

26 Though *able* to make anything at all, God will not *wish to* make anything below His own standards: --He cannot be tempted with evil according to James 1,13, and Evil, not being an Absolute, is therefore sub-standard!

27 and *if* this *is* the case, then ultimate reality is *Personal*, not Material.

28 1 John 4,8. If God is love, then it follows that creatures in His image will be love too.

29 Love presupposes personality. Not that animals cannot love, but theirs is a different function.

30 Sub-creation is a concept found in Tolkien; see http://library.taylor.edu/dotAsset/afcf88aa-52b7-4dda-8e6b-d5efd2e6b1f6.pdf

31 (Didn't God know already? Presumably, but as Kierkegaard points out in *Philosophiske Smuler* where he attacks Hegelianism: in a sense you cannot know what *is* going to be chosen until it actually is.)

32 "Rejoice, young man, during your childhood, and let your heart be pleasant during the days of young manhood. And follow the impulses of your heart and the desires of your eyes. Yet know that God will bring you to judgment for all these things". Ecclesiastes 11.9
- *New American Standard Version* (1995)

33 (The impression one may get from Environmentalist pressure-groups. They often seem to have an anti-human emphasis. "We should all gracefully bow ourselves off the stage, become extinct, and leave Nature to clean up the mess.")

34 (-implied, as I see it-) he is placed in a garden Hebrew גן in an area called Eden. The word means an enclosed garden, and is connected to a verb meaning "defend" (Online Bible Hebrew Lexicon http://www.eliyah.com/lexicon.html) also http://www.blueletterbible.org/lang/lexicon/lexicon.cfm?Strongs=H1588&t=KJV . When translated into Greek in the Septuagint they used the word: paradeison –Paradise. Protected environments for the inception of life are so commonplace in nature that they are practically the norm, one very obvious example is the egg, another the womb.

There is also the possible implication that the creation of the adam did not happen in the Garden, but it was placed there afterwards: "and there He put the man whom He *had formed*" (the verb is in the perfect tense, in other words the formation was already completed).

35 Outside the Garden of Eden the environment could be a very different matter - perhaps even hostile until tamed. Humankind is told to "subdue" the earth in Genesis 1,28) cf. Micah 7,19 *"He will subdue our iniquities"*.

36 Michelsen, Leif M. Fortolkning til Første Mosebok Oslo 1972. p.58 commentary on v 18. Lutherstiftelsens Forlag; Lunde Forlag. ISBN 82 531 0634 8

37 These have also been formed in the same way as the human and also have "the breath of life" so they are similar to the Man, but the Man is the leader, and therefore defines the environment by *giving names to them* Genesis 2,20 New International Version.

Ecclesiastes 3:19. "Man's fate is like that of the animals; the same fate awaits them both: As one dies, so dies the other. All have the same breath; {Or spirit} man has no advantage over the animal."

38 In a figure of speech, naturally. I am aware that technically and scientifically it actually means the opposite of colloquial usage. http://en.wikipedia.org/wiki/Quantum_leap

39 Woman is built from side of the man, however, that does not necessarily establish superiority but equality; had she been under him, near-eastern culture would be more likely to have made her from a bone of Adam's foot!

Were *he* built from her, all human life would come through her exclusively; Because she is built from him, all human life comes from them *jointly*: -"All the families of the earth" each with their own validity, and later in Genesis, all are intended to be blessed with the blessing of Abraham (Genesis 12,3).

Genesis is, in fact, written in the cultural context of a variety of tribes, cultures and civilisations, from the memories of Ebla, of the Mesopotamian civilisations, to Egypt the great power of the ancient world. Much of the book is about the origins of the different groups and explaining their variety and common origin.

⁴⁰ Genesis 1, 24 and 5,1 There is nothing to say that two people of the same sex cannot enter into some kind of contract identical in conditions to matrimony. If they want to they can, but marriage it is not.

Woman plus Man are meant to become something greater when united than they are apart, gain greater scope, range and properties like two elements forming a new chemical substance when they combine. Similarly, you need a left and a right leg to walk, two ears to sense direction, two eyes to sense distance and see things in the round. As the old saying goes: "two heads are better than one".

Like + like produces more of the same: Marriage can therefore never be two people of the same sex. If it is two of the same sex, it cannot be marriage; if it is marriage it cannot be two of the same gender. A same-sex marriage is a contradiction in terms.

National legislatures do not have the power to turn the moon into green-cheese by issuing a law, or get the universe to stand on its head, or change the essence of marriage by redefining it. Even if 100% of the world population agreed -which they don't! it would still be in the minority since God is infinite and understands far better than we how human-beings are put together and function.

Therefore, laws treating marriage on a gender-neutral basis are not regulating marriage, but doing something else: re-defining marriage and shoving an Orwellian-Newspeak definition down our throats as if we were Strasbourg geese, and lampooning us and declaring us intolerant if we fail to swear to the politically correct creed.

41 If humans existed purely for the purpose of having children, then we would have to ask "why do our children exist, then?" But if they only exist so they can have children, too, why will those children exist, then? And if those children only will exist to have children, why.... ? And so on ad infinitum. In the end one has to arrive at a place where and when people exist for some other reason than bringing forth the next generation.

Neither Woman nor Man exist merely to have babies. All of us exist for our own sake: to be loved and blessed by God and be at the receiving end of His Love. And because He loves us, He has given us the privilege and pure joy of passing His Love on, and being the material expression for others of God's smile; for creature that love will find their joy and fulfilment in giving love. "*It is more blessed to give than to receive*" sit. Jesus of Nazareth, quoted Acts 20,35

Our raison d'être is independent of reproduction. We exist in our own right and have the privilege of fulfilling and accomplishing many other things too.

42 For the concept of the collective image of God, I must acknowledge my indebtedness to Lance Lambert.

43 (The Nicene Creed). She is no mere appendage. The way God went about making her was designed to illustrate the inner consistency of the trinity: the male is the origin, and in the image of God; the female springs forth from the male, and is equally in the image of God. The child springs from both, and is equally in the image of God. This is in the same way that God the Father is fully God and "Is-that-He-Is", God the Holy Spirit is fully God "as He does and says", God the Son is fully God "as He shows Himself to be. All these aspects of God are totally one and the same. Nor is the Holy Spirit "the female principle of the Godhead" – that would violate the very principle of Trinity three in ONE. It would make it diversity in One, which is not then the principal Athanasius was expressing.

God **transcends** gender, which is a created thing and therefore He cannot be divided up into male and female; Also: The Holy Spirit is specifically spoken of as "He" in John 16, even though the Greek word for "spirit" takes neutral grammatical gender.

44 "Adam" is masculine gender noun in Hebrew so when it is used collectively it does not just refer to males.

45 Perfection, in the Genesis description, is not the homogenous, white, unchanging, infinite and totally uniform sphere of Parmenides the Greek philosopher, -and what one notes is that though Parmenides' description was not accepted, his presupposition of the uniformity and unity of perfection was. Perfection in the Bible description is not the Greek "antitype" of which all other products to a greater or lesser degree are failed editions. Greek perfectionism is a useful tool, but like only having the <u>end-view projection</u> out of the <u>three projections</u> of a technical drawing. It does not give your a view of the object in the round. A proper grasp of perfection has to emanate from an acquaintance with the Infinite all-encompassing God, not from a mental projection of the philosopher. "The God of the Bible and the god found in philosophy are not the same." verbatim cit. Svein Rise, systematic theologian at NLA.

The Greek pursuit of perfection has produced some splendid results, but also some pernicious ones such as becoming the premise for eugenics and genocide.

Parmenides: Greek philosopher of Elea in southern Italy born c. 515 BC. (2009). Encyclopædia Britannica. *Encyclopædia Britannica 2009 Ultimate Reference Suite.* Chicago: Encyclopædia Britannica.

46 or were even killed for not fitting in (e.g. if they were girls, or Spartan babies that didn't measure up.)

47 Like the constant variety of a fractal image. (see: **complexity.** (2009). Encyclopædia Britannica. Encyclopædia Britannica 2009 Ultimate Reference Suite. Chicago: Encyclopædia Britannica.

48 Ecclesiastes 3:11 NIV 1984

49 (Not that we have arrived at an *adequate* grasp of evil, but we *have* made a start; see discussion below)

50 Good-and-Evil, (hebrew: tov ra) is in principal a philosophical concept, not a literal tree as such, although that concept has become - unfortunately - a horrible reality, and as such it is literal, too.

51 "Fruit trees" in ancient agriculture were important resources. From them you got figs, dates, grapes, olive oil, pomegranates and shade. When speaking figuratively of trees, then, you find them talked of as qualities and the place where you obtained things: "fatness" (the olive tree) "sweetness" (the fig tree) much in the way we use the words "source, or origin". Wisdom is called a "tree of life" (Proverbs 3:18 *She is a tree of life to them that lay hold upon her: and happy is every one that retaineth her*.); kingdoms are visualized as "trees"; love is spoken of as the taste of sweet fruit; children are born under them. Never anywhere, though, will you find a reference to a ~~tree of knowledge.~~

52 "Knowledge", in Genesis is "first-hand experience" and "personal acquaintance" not simply "accumulating facts".

53 The invitation would otherwise be meaningless (cf. also, the naming of the animals).

54 Besides which, each choice changed Perfection into a new Perfection. The "road not taken" was therefore an irrelevant consideration, for nothing "better" had been lost in the development, as every choice was equally good, equally valid. In any case one had all eternity to try out the other possibilities.

55 Genesis 2,17 "you shall die, dying"

56 That would be to read the prudery of a far later age into an ancient, ancient story. Even the most perfunctory reading of the Bible shows that sex was a positive thing and not the forbidden fruit. Apart from being commanded (!) on the 6th day (Genesis 1:28) we can also point to the example of Enoch:

Enoch lived 365 years; his first child was born when he was 65, and he "walked with God" for 300 years. The implication is that his walk with God began when his first child was born. We also learn that he "begat sons and daughters", in short, that he had an active sex-life while he walked with God. And Enoch walked (i.e. "lived his life") in such close fellowship that the Lord took him so he did not die. Therefore an active sex-life (within marriage) and a busy family life are NO hindrance to a close walk with God! (Genesis 5:21-23)

57 Knowledge *per se* is consistently positive in the Old Testament. The horrendous misnomer 'The Tree of Knowledge' has misled readers to jump to completely wrong conclusions: that God wanted to repress us and keep us ignorant; it underlies the misconception that enquiring minds must turn their backs on religion and that science and faith are at war. As if we could ever get too clever for God! As if the Creator of the Universe with its multi-trillions of galaxies could ever feel threatened by what we could invent or discover! The whole idea is an absurdity; a half-breed intrusion picked up from Greek mythology (cf Prometheus).

58 pardon the Canadianism, - I *was* born there after all! :-)

59 I say that as a figure of speech. You don't *really* "become what you eat". Your food changes into you.

60 Not that Eve and Adam understood *what* they were not choosing, but they did understand they were *not* to choose it; negating their own love of God was a precondition of the act itself!

61 Which is why the tree of knowing-good-and-evil is also a reflection of our free will: Love and free will are two sides of the same coin.

62 This will still follow if we accept the traditional interpretation of the tree: that it was the choice to decide for *oneself* what was good or bad (thereby inventing our own absolutes), and not let God decide. One cannot decide for oneself what is good and what is evil when every choice is good and there is no evil. The forbidden choice still implies a prohibition to manufacture evil and destroy perfection.

63 (whatever "theory" must be like on God's plane of existence), cf. also Proverbs 15,11

64 For God is the only being in existence able to make a truly existential choice, with no reference to any criteria but His own, ("Hayah esher Hayah" – I AM that I AM, Exodus 3,14) and God has chosen to be what He IS -Love.

65 - unlike the Greek gods!

66 John 14:15; 1 John 5:3

67 This is only part of the story, of course. Another aspect, (and there are certainly many others beyond this one,) is that being created for fellowship with other people, we take our self-image from the feedback we get from them. But we give, and get, self-centred feedback, which creates insecurities and anxieties which leads to even greater self-preoccupation. In short, ego-ism, as opposed to a healthy self-love, sours very quickly and becomes destructive.

68 Genesis 3:7

69 Genesis 3:22. You notice that every single human being, has these three experiences in common -even the unborn! They all experience some form of **good** (even if no more than the brief comfort of a mother's womb), they all experience some form of **evil**, and they all experience **death**. And all of these are en-tailed in the statement in Genesis "*of the tree of the knowing of good and evil you shall not eat for in the day that you eat of it, dying you shall die*" (2,17)

70 http://www.str.org/site/News2?page=NewsArticle&id=5124 Remarks by John Milton and Augustine's view were the start-ing-point of my way of reading the Creation Story. The reader must decide for them self whether I have read it correctly, or read something into it that is not there.

71 (The idea that humankind was never meant to take the com-mand seriously is an indirect way of calling God a liar! cf. He-brews 6:18 and John 8:44)

72 1 John 1,5 The alternative to this would be dualism: an eter-nal struggle of equal and opposite forces of good and evil. Ac-cording to this view, if God is infinite goodness, then He will have to be opposed by an infinite evil force and Good will never triumph over evil. Clearly the bible does not uphold this view: Isaiah 44,6 & 8; 45,5,6 & 21

73 cit. from Julian of Norwich, *Revelations of Divine Love*, chapter 86.

74 It is our assertion that the prime reason for creating our Universe was joy: the proliferation of Happiness. Being Love, our God wished to give His love to His creation, not just to Himself, even though that would be enough for Him since His infinite love would have been given to an infinite object. We exist so that we can be the recipients of His love; bathe in His smile for ever and radiate it to all around us.

75 Without Love the universe would ultimately just be a gigantic toy, a plaything for His omnipotence but not a wonderful interplay of joyful relationships.

76*"For a little while I have whirled you up out of the dust so that you might be to the praise of My glory. It is no small privilege that I have done this thing for the dust that is you."* (Word intimated to me -on recollecting dust caught in a sunbeam- by the Lord ca. 2008). Not just for the sake of the job, of course, but for our own sakes too: to put us at the receiving end of all that love.

77 Some muslim theologians have objected to God being Love on the grounds that this would restrict His absolute freedom of choice. It does not, it simply reveals to us what that choice *is*.

78 For a good discussion of the different words for love in Ancient Greek see Lewis, C.S. "The Four Loves" New York 1960 ISBN 0-15-132916-8

79 The language common to (*lingua franca* of) most of the Roman Empire around about the beginning of the Christian Era, functioning like International English does today. Koiné was used as a first language by many, and as a second language by other national and ethnic groups to communicate with each other. Latin took on this role in Western Europe in Medieval times, while Greek continued to be the language of the Eastern Roman Empire, (and sometimes was replaced by Arabic).

80 1 Corinthians 13:4-8 New English Translation; http://bible.org/netbible/index.htm

81 (eternal life is a **quality** more than it is a quantity)

82 God *is* knowable, if He sovereignly chooses to make Himself known!

83 1 John 4:7&8 "Dear friends, let us love one another, for love comes from God. Everyone who loves has been born of God and knows God. Whoever does not love does not know God, because God is love." John 17:3 "Now this is eternal life: that they know you, the only true God, and Jesus Christ, whom you have sent." Both cit. from http://www.biblegateway.com/

84 it follows that if the origin of all things is personal, relationship with that person will be presumably be key to a correct relationship to the universe.

85 http://www.creeds.net/Westminster/shorter_catechism.html The Westminster Shorter Catechism1647

86 for example, when we have used penicillin to defeat pathogens, we have realised rather late in the day just how important our flora of intestinal bacteria are, or that they constitute an integral part of us. So our well-intentioned penicillin has had to some rather negative side-effects. Another example is plastics becoming a vast ocean of pollution.

87 Genesis 6:5

88 The doctrine of 'total depravity' does not mean that everything about human beings is bad. It means that the bad makes its influence known in every aspect of our nature, also our better and more lovable ones. On the other had the good will have a similar influence on the bad sides. A good illustration is the vicious bomb-attack on the 22nd of July 2011 in Oslo, Norway followed by the cold-blooded massacre on Utøya of 66 young people, the injury of 69 others and the traumatisation of many more (one of whom was my pupil). **The deed was vile; the collective response of the people of Norway a thing of great beauty.** The existence of good and evil in everyone, which is a truism, may also remind one of Manichaeism, but with an important difference: you can never defeat the evil within by separating yourself from it. This can only be done by restoring the missing element, - which will then brings about a healing (redemption) of the entire individual.

89 (-as it says in Proverbs: "*Folly leads conduct astray, yet it is against the Lord that the heart rages*") Proverbs 19,3 cit. from http://www.catholic.org/bible/book.php?id=24 New Jerusalem Bible. I have exchanged the name of God for "the Lord" to avoid offence.

⁹⁰ So there is no point in comparing yourself with anyone else and thinking you are no worse than they are. Even the very best of us are not good enough anyway!

⁹¹ 2 Corinthians 6:14 cit Blue Letter Bible blueletterbible.org

⁹² e.g prostitution. We note that the other forms of love, are all directed "horizontally", so to speak, to creatures on the same plane as ourselves; Agapé love, with its direct affinity to the nature of God, has a "vertical" dimension, with a being on a higher plane. This is similar to the distinction made in James 3,15 between wisdom from above, and earthly wisdom.

⁹³ Gen 5,3

⁹⁴ Ephesians 2, 4-5

⁹⁵ Romans 8, 22 οἴδαμεν γὰρ ὅτι πᾶσα ἡ κτίσις συστενάζει καὶ συνωδίνει ἄχρι τοῦ νῦν

⁹⁶ Love, being an absolute quality of God, cannot be defined exhaustively. The passage in 1 Corinthians 13, 4-7 does not so much tell us what love is, as tell us how love *acts*.

⁹⁷ He Himself is the only being in existence capable of a truly existential choice. All other beings exist within a frame given by the conditions of their creation. God is His own framework, and therefore can be what or whoever He chooses, - and He has made His choice: 1 John 4,8.

⁹⁸ (or even unintentionally)

⁹⁹ Which is why the Nazis picked on Jews, Gypsies and homosexuals.

[100] Such committal is almost invariably cloaked in some form of self-aggrandisement, disguised under the mask of some "noble cause" legitimising the suffering that follows, and portraying the perpetrator as a hero or martyr. So Genghis Khan believed himself mandated by the gods to unite mankind into one great empire, and the train of wars he set in motion is calculated to have cost as many as 40 million lives   an equal number to WW2. http://necrometrics.com/pre1700a.htm#20worst -at a time when the world population was possibly 450 million (https://en.wikipedia.org/wiki/World_population). This was a mere fraction of the estimated 2300 million world population in 1940 which was the next conflagration to claim an equal number of dead.

[101] or believe the abusive words hurled at us by dysfunctional parents and teachers, which then become self-fulfilling prophecies. Like the punk-rockers: They were so used to being called "punks" and "rotten" by grown-ups, that they made a virtue of it and formed a culture from it and became all the things their elders were telling them they were! No surprise one of their trend-setters called himself "Johnny Rotten".

[102] This is a possibility so harsh that academic society prefers not to consider it, for then the capacity to make the same choice lies within us all, and then some people are criminals by choice, not just a victim of upbringing and environment and the Social System. But evil patently *is* often chosen as a form of self-assertion; for example, it is a central dynamic in football hooliganism.

[103] Not that the Lord needs to do that much, --just let evil run its course; the negative fruits will come of themselves.

[104] John 13,27 Blue Letter Bible NIV.

[105] Isaiah 45,7

[106] Jeremaiah 7,31.

[107] cf. Acts 4, 26.28

[108] 1 Corinthians 2,8

109 (Hebrews 12,11) On a deep level, they are drawn into "the fellowship of His sufferings" (see discussion in part following). "For godly grief produces a repentance that leads to salvation without regret, whereas worldly grief produces death" 2 Corinthians 7:10 English Standard Version. cit. blueletter-bible.org

110 No individual planned, for example, the slums and squalor of the new cities arising in the wake of the Industrial Revolution, nor were they very different from the abysmal squalor the rural poor lived in at the time. (When they idealised rural life, the Romantics were *criticised* by contemporaries for burying their head in the sand.) The rural poor were so impoverished that one farmer paid 10 workers to dig up his field for sowing - because it was cheaper than oats for the horse that would have been used to plough it! (source BBC Open University).

The new factory owners were simply following their own noses and making use of an economic opportunity. The spin off effects arose gradually and unexpectedly.

Adam Smith did not predict this kind of thing when writing "The Wealth of Nations", but presupposed that natural forces left un-reined will bring about exclusively positive results. Living in the Age of Enlightenment he inherited a concept of God's Providence that was by then stripped of its central presupposition: that Providence is an aspect of an individual relationship to God (Romans 8,28) not a general rule that we live in "the best of all possible worlds".

The "Wealth of Nations" is furthermore read out context, it is contended that it was a part of his whole moral philosophy and has to be read in the light of it. *"Adam Smith's philosophy bears little resemblance to the libertarian caricature put forth by proponents of laissez faire markets who describe humans solely as* homo economicus. *For Smith, the market is a mechanism of morality and social support."* https://www.iep.utm.edu/smith/.

111 Naturally the negative effects of impersonal systems will be further compounded when some of the individuals are driven by personal and evil intentions: greed, love of money, tax-evasion, scams, profiteering or elaborate economic deceptions such as insider-trading.

[112] Peer Gynt Act 3 scene 3. The quotation is from R. Farquharson Sharp's translation and more clearly to my point than Ibsen's wording: *"Å ja; det svir til de skyldfri, sa'e fanden, moer hans gav ham hug, for faer hans var fuld!"*

http://www.archive.org/stream/peergyntdramaticooib-
seuoft/peergyntdramaticooibseuoft_djvu.txt

The innocent are also victims of their own goodness. Not being committed to evil themselves, they cannot imagine or take seriously what evil people are capable of doing; -until it happens! So not being forewarned, they are not forearmed and evil strikes them unprepared. Nor are the good prepared to answer the evil in kind, but if they do, can risk becoming evil themselves!

[113] Suggest there might be intelligent life elsewhere in the universe, and intellectuals applaud; Suggest that there might be such a thing as *angels*, and some intellectuals jeer, and think they are being very clever: I remember Dr. Martin Lloyd Jones being ridiculed on the BBC on just such a score!

[114] -ben elohim – Genesis 6, 2&4; Job 1,6 & 2,1

[115] Job 38, 4&7. The most likely explanation of this is that these were angels, especially if Satan is among them, since he later on in the tale displays non-human powers. Another alternative given for "sons of God" according to Jewish tradition, instead of angels, is the offspring of Seth. (Source: Megan Easley-Walsh.)

[116] A Discourse, by President Joseph Smith (Joseph Smith Jnr.) Delivered at the Conference held near the Temple, in Nauvoo, April 6, 1844 Reported by W. Richards, W. Woodruff, T. Bullock, and W. Clayton.

"Intelligence is eternal and exists upon a self-existent principle. It is a spirit from age to age, and there is no creation about it. All the minds and spirits that God ever sent into the world are susceptible of enlargement.   The first principles of man are self-existent with God. God himself, finding he was in the midst of spirits and glory, because he was more intelligent, saw proper to institute laws whereby the rest could have a privilege to advance like himself." *Journal of Discourses, Volume 6, pages 1-11.* sit. http://www.truthandgrace.com/joesinner.html

[117] Pullman, Philip The Amber Spyglass, Scholastic Uk Ltd 2000 p. 210: *"You say that so casually" she said "as if it were something I should know too, but.. How can it be? The Authority created the worlds didn't he? He existed before everything. How can he have come into being?" "This is angelic knowledge" said Ogonwe. "It shocked some of us too to learn that the Authority (i.e. God —ed.) is not the creator. There may have been a creator, or there may not: we don't know. All we know is that at some point the Authority took charge.." "the Authority first set himself above the rest of the angels"* p.211 .

In Pullman's defence, he never claims the cosmology of his trilogy to be more than fantasy. Statements about non-existent things can be considered true, false, or neither, for they treat of things which are not.

His claim is purely atheistic: that neither God nor any other spirit exists. *"..I saw there wasn't any God at all and that physics was more interesting. The Christian religion is a very powerful mistake, that's all"* p.442.

[118] Cf. Revelation 4,11

[119] though God's enemies will always go in for as destructive perversions of truth as possible.

[120] (which arbitrarily exalts relativism itself to an absolute). However, "everything is relative", simply means "the sum of all things is the absolute, and I am a small corner of it". As everything must needs include God, there *are* absolutes as God is Absolute; Even His absence defines Evil.

[121] John Milton, Paradise Lost, London 1674. Book 1 lines 37-41 & 589-598. The latter extract was the original hermeneutical key that led to this book. http://www.dartmouth.edu/~milton/reading_room/pl/book_1/

[122] it is *our* enemy, though, as it was not intended for us. We were created for perpetuality. 1 Cor. 15,26 *"The last enemy that will be destroyed is death"*

[123] (having a beginning and end, - even if that end be the end of time itself)

[124] (an endlessly repeated cycle). All created things have a beginning and are therefore not eternal. If they carry on for ever and ever it is because they has a beginning but not an end. Eternity exists outside of time, while perpetuality exists *within* time.

I have had to coin a word not found in the dictionary, as the word that is, "perpetuity" would be ambiguous here and language is a tool, not a dictator. When the tool functions inadequately for a new kind of job, you have to devise refinements. So Jeremy Bentham invented the word "International" -and thank goodness he did! In my own defence: Saying that only words found in the dictionary are permissible is like accepting that "Everything not compulsory is forbidden".

[125] http://en.wikipedia.org/wiki/Mayfly or http://da.wikipedia.org/wiki/Døgnflue where we are told that many of these only live at the adult stage for a few hours!

[126] i.e, things created to be ephemeral. Their life-cycle is their form of perpetual life.

[127] cf Michelsen, Leif M. <u>Fortolkning til Første Mosebok</u> Oslo 1972 p 54. "The Tree of Life has this name because the tree is able to give life through its fruit. The background is v.7 and humanity's mortality. Humankind does not seem to have absolute immortality before the fall: the clear underlining of commonality with the earth prevents us from thinking otherwise. But humankind had a relative and conditional .. immortality, that in the account is expressed through their relationship to the tree of life and the command. When it says in 3,22 that the tree will give eternal life it is not necessarily to be understood that humankind would receive a qualitatively different life than they had before. It can mean that the life they already had will continue for an extremely long period. The tree would then have a life-sustaining function. By living near the tree and eating of it humankind could keep death at a distance and live. The verbal forms of 3,22 can be construed this way. To be driven away from the tree therefore becomes a sentence of death. There seems to be no sign of a distinction between physical and spiritual death in the Story. That the tree of life is not hedged in by a prohibition shows that God has intended humankind to have free access to the tree, as long as it lives in obedience to and trust in Him." (translation from the Norwegian, my own).

[128] Genesis 2,17 The translation of *"for in the day that you eat of it you shall surely die."* has the footnote"Heb. *dying thou shalt die"* in the Oxford edition of the Authorised Version. the Hebrew phrase מוֹת תָּמוּת

(http://www.blueletterbible.org/Bible.cfm?b=Gen&c=2&v=7&t=NKJV#conc/17) (transliteration *mō·wṯ tā·mūṯ* http://biblos.com/genesis/2-17.htm). The verb *mō·wṯ* is infinitive in the first word and imperfect in the next and seems to cover death as a process and an event.

[129] 1 Peter 5,8. As a curiosity: Voldemort in the <u>Harry Potter</u> series is a name meaning "thief of death". The evil wizard maintains his life by incarcerating part of his own soul in some external object (called a "horcrux") and has to take another person's life in order for the spell to work. The resonance here is possibly due to J.K.Rowling's deeply Christian world-view, which underlies, but is not up-fronted in her book.

[130] Julian of Norwich, Revelations of Divine Love, ch. 86

131 (and not the logic of advanced biology or mechanics) cf C.S.Lewis Reflections on the Psalms.

132 This is best summed up in His self-description in Exodus: "*I Am that I Am*" a phrase which in Hebrew can be taken in a number of ways, but the interpretations indicate His self-determining yet unchanging nature: He-is-and-will-continue-to-be what He-is-and-will-continue-to-be".

What He has chosen to be is of course beyond human description, the only adequate one being the one He Himself gave: "*I AM that I AM*" (Exodus 3,14). It is the only expression that covers His every quality. His Name YWHW (*He Is*) may be considered His self-description. See: http:// e n . w i k i p e d i a . o r g / w i k i / Names_of_God_in_Judaism#The_Tetragrammaton; (http://biblicalhebrew.org/hebrew-names-of-god-in-the-bible.aspx) http://www.jstor.org/discover/10.2307/1515709? uid=3738744&uid=2129&uid=2&uid=70&uid=4&sid=47698 820306447

133 Love is voluntary. It cannot be forced or bribed. Song of Songs 8,

134 Proverbs 17:12; Hebrews 1:9

135 The consequences of evil cannot be avoided as long as evil continues to exist. Matthew 18,7 ""*Woe to the world because of the things that cause people to sin! Such things must come, but woe to the man through whom they come!*" Our thesis is, of course that the eradication of evil is the long-term purpose, but for our sakes, His purpose must come through a process, not a drastic obliteration.

136 God alone knows how many there are. I have only listed some instances, not an exhaustive survey.

137 Psalm 136, all the way through, among other examples.

138 He still loves us for what we originally meant to be, and because of what He will make of us if He, the potter, is allowed to re-work our clay. "*Lord -if you exist- take me, shape me, mould me according to Your will.*" *15th February 1969*

139 Genesis 6:5

140 Life on land, -not marine life, of course. (This is so obvious that we actually never think of it!).

141 But the three *wives* of Shem, Ham and Japheth were *not* the children of Noah and his wife, so though our male lineage converges on Noah and his wife, our female lineage has a much earlier figure in common: - Eve! It is interesting to hear that DNA research also indicates that our common female ancestor is of greater antiquity than our common male ancestor.

142 Genesis 8:21; Many have made much of this curse (mentioned as part of God's judgement in Genesis 3:17). They seem, however, to overlook the fact that Genesis says the curse was <u>withdrawn</u> after the Flood!

143 Pain is a life-saver! Leprosy, for example, is a disease that attacks the surface muscles of the skin and desensitizes the sense of touch so the leper does not feel pain. As a result, a person with leprosy may walk about with a stone in their shoe and not feel it. Instead of taking out the stone, they continue to walk on it and a sore develops on the sole of their foot. Not knowing the sore is there, this develops into an infection, and they end up losing their leg, or if they are even more unlucky, get blood-poisoning (sepsis). Leprosy does not normally kill people. Sepsis often does.

144 2 Thessalonians 2:7; It does not say who/what the hindrance is, or who/what will cause its removal. By way of an aside: God may sometimes also intervene to hinder some of humankind's more idiotic projects from coming to fruition (cf the tower of Babel).

145 St John's Revelations is not the main focus of this book. Where we are at in the process right now is anybody's guess, but we have clearly not got to the end.

[146] Romans 13:1-7, especially verse 4. The role of governments as "deacons" (gk: *diakonoi*) is that of a representative with the job of performing a task on behalf of someone else and in the same way the other person would have done it. Our loyalty to governments is therefore not absolute, but conditional to them being God's representatives and not his enemies. For this reason, opposition to Adolf Hitler was not in conflict with Christian ethics. cf Psalm 94:20 "Shall the throne of iniquity have fellowship with thee, which frameth mischief by a law?" See: Exelby, Richard Mure: The Deacons' Assignment in the Light of the New Testament Material, Bergen 1997 pages 58 & 59 (M.A. thesis in Christian Studies Norwegian Teaching Academy)

[147] Genesis 3:6

[148] On the contrary, they must be good, as God created us that way. They are impaired though, and thereby part and parcel of the interwoven good-and-evil we became (cf. Romans 1:21)

[149] Proverbs 2:6 & 9:4 In fact a large part of the Bible (Job, Psalms, Proverbs, Ecclesiastes and Song of Songs) are collectively known as "The Wisdom Books".

[150] (there are, of course, a large number of others). Paul, who had rabbinical training, mentions the Law in our hearts Romans 2:15 The moot point with others Law systems (for example Hammurabi or Confucius/K'ung-fu-tzu) is to what degree they have their source in God's wisdom, or in fallible human sources; in many cases, no doubt a bit of both.

[151] Leviticus 19:18

[152] Cf. Deuteronomy 24:1-4 and Malachi 2:14-16

[153] This is a truism so obvious it hardly needs embroidering. However, as stating the obvious does no harm, let us note that just simple adherence to "you shall not steal" would have enormous consequences. Doors would never be locked – or even have locks; car-keys would become a thing of the past. The same is true of "you shall not commit adultery": within a generation Clamydia, Gonorrhoea, Syphilis and AIDS would become very rare diseases.

[154] even though the Law itself is (Psalm 19:3).

155 As long as the world was was perfect, all decisions were equally valid and therefore ethically correct. We can hardly begin to imagine how different things would have been if we had never fallen.

156 Not that I wish to suggest that the conscience is merely an emotional response. The jury is still out on the issue of what the conscience is exactly.

157 "Tolerating the Intolerable" was a phrase used by Emporer Hirohito when he announced the Japanese surrender at the end of the 2nd World War. Hasegawa, Tsuyoshi *Racing the enemy: Stalin, Truman, and the surrender of Japan* p. 240 Harvard 2005. All honour to Hirohito, who one-sidedly ignored his generals and drew the war to a close rather than see his people suffer even longer.

158 To grasp how this can be, you have to understand what the teaching on the Trinity is about.
"I Am that I Am" said God to Moses. God's self-description covers every quality of the Almighty, but it will take more than eternity to perceive all that is included in it.
"God the Father" is <u>God as HE IS</u>.
"God the Holy Spirit" is <u>God as HE IS when He is present</u>.
"God the Son" is <u>God as HE IS seen to be</u>.
It is always a case of One **God** as HE IS. God is One in a Threefold Unity.

Jesus showed us Who God Is, but did not live as God while here. He stayed within the parameters of human existence. That does not mean God's power was no longer active, but that it was God's *Nature* that was being demonstrated on earth in the human Son of Man.

159 It was not a mistake on God's part to create us Love, and thereby indirectly let Evil become possible -far from it! Love is the best thing He could possibly chosen to make us. But since we made the mistake of choosing good-and-evil, God took the responsibility for us letting us have that choice. But it was necessary, as I have already explained.

160 c.f. Genesis 6:6-: "And the LORD was sorry that He had made man on the earth, and He was grieved in His heart." There is an objective and a subjective side to the atonement: Objectively, the full payment was made for all the consequences and penalty of evil. Subjectively, we see the misery the Fall has caused God Himself. How tolerating us fallen creatures is living torture for Him.

161 cf Revelation 13:8 & 1Pe 1:19, 20; On God's own sorrow see Genesis 6:6: "And the LORD was sorry that He had made man on the earth, and He was grieved in His heart." cf. the Hebrew verb נָחַם in Niphal tense, for "regret, rue, repent," and עָצַב http://www.blueletterbible.org/ lexicon

162 1 John 2:2

163 John 19,30 Christ's final words on the Cross. Because Evil is not an absolute, it is not infinite, and therefore it can be brought to a conclusion.

164 (one of the possible ways to translate John 10:17)
   http://www.blueletterbible.org/Bible.cfm?
b=Jhn&c=1&v=17&t=KJV#vrsn/5

165 "In vain the firstborn seraph tries to sound the depths of love divine." (Charles Wesley).

166 (A standard parallel drawn from Leviticus 25:47-55, and referred to in Galatians 4:5 and Titus 2:14)

167 Song of Songs 8:6. 1 Corinthians 15:54. "Death is swallowed up in victory--In *Hebrew* of Isa 25:8 , from which it is quoted, "*He* (Jehovah) *will swallow up* death in victory"; that is, *for ever:* as "in victory" often means in *Hebrew* idiom (Jer 3:5 Lam 5:20). Christ will swallow it up *so altogether victoriously* that it shall never more regain its power (compare Hsa 6:2 13:14 2Cr 5:4 Hbr 2:14, 15 Rev 20:14 21:4)." Verbatim from Fausset, A.R. The First Epistle of Paul the Apostle to the Corinthians sit from: www.blueletterbible.org/commentaries... 1Cr_15_54

168 Romans 5:5.

[169] John 3:3 The term γεννηθῇ ἄνωθεν "Or *from above*; the Greek is purposely ambiguous and can mean both *again* and *from above*; also verse 7" see: English Standared Version cit: http://www.blueletterbible.org/Bible.cfm?b=Jhn&c=3&v=5&t=KJV#vrsn/3

[170] H*ristos Voskrese! - Vaistinu Voskrese!* Christ is Risen! He is risen indeed;

[171] just as the point of being at Perfection is to stay there, so the point of coming to Christ is to abide in Him.

[172] This, in my view is the context in which we must construe the description of humankind as "Saint and sinner" *"Luther described Christians as "simultaneously saint and sinner." Some religious traditions distinguish between "saints," who obey God's will, and "sinners," who disobey. Lutherans cling to a both/and understanding of Christian identity that redefines the word "saint": a saint is a forgiven sinner. Our dual identity as saints and sinners reminds us that our righteousness always depends on God's grace, never on our own religious behaviour. At the same time, our recognition that sin, while forgiven, remains a powerful force in the world and in ourselves gives us a realistic ability to confront cruelty and evil, confident that God will have the last word."* (NB: I am not a Lutheran, I just happen to agree with him on this point).

see: http://www.thelutheran.org/article/article.cfm?article_id=5895&key=34751023

[173] -it is even termed "kondisionalis" in Norwegian grammar. For Greek usage consider http://www.ntgreek.org/learn_nt_-greek/subj-detail-frame.htm "The action of the verb will possibly happen, depending on certain objective factors or circumstances. It has a number of specific uses and is oftentimes used in conditional statements (i.e. 'If...then...' clauses) or in purpose clauses."

[174] For you are encountering God Himself, -the Holy Spirit, through His Word.

[175] so He is the the active agent, you are the passive recipient. But if you reject it, your rejection is an active response made on your part.

[176] Romans 10:9, cf Psalm 145,8. & Psalm 94:9: "Does he who fashioned the ear not hear? Does he who formed the eye not see?" (NIV) https://www.blueletterbible.org/kjv/psa/94/9/ t_bibles_572009

[177] 1 John 3:8 RSV

[178] Judges 16:17 Samson's real failing was of course, that he did not understand the *true* source of his power. If he had said to Delilah "the source of my power is the Spirit of God that comes upon me and gives med superhuman strength" there is nothing she or the Philistines could have done about it.

[179] If errors they be. Many things have been erroneously banned from standard English that actually are legitimate: the split infinitive and the double-negative among other things. As to English spelling -people have been complaining about its idiosyncrasies since the late Middle Ages so the less said the better. I pay it all due lip-service and pragmatic attention, but still maintain it makes no sense. English slings together the spelling-systems of about 10 different languages without any adequate harmonisation between them, -and are we supposed to stand in awe of the result?!